David C. Cook Foundation Monographs
C. Lawrence Brook, Editor

This monograph series is intended for Christian communicators involved in the media worldwide. The series addresses various facets of communication, cross-cultural research, and prominent issues related to publishing and other media.

Understanding Pictures in Papua New Guinea

Bruce L. Cook

 David C. Cook Foundation   Elgin, Illinois USA

Note: References to scholarly studies have generally been omitted from this monograph. Those interested in pursuing the subject in more depth should consult the author's dissertation, "Understanding Pictures in Papua New Guinea, 1975: An Experiment Comparing Style and Content in Sociological, Epistemological, and Cognitive Context." Copies can be obtained for a small fee from University Microfilms International, P.O. Box 1764, Ann Arbor, Michigan 48106, USA. Publication Number: 79-10, 041. For further questions about the monograph, write to the David C. Cook Foundation, 850 N. Grove Ave., Elgin, Illinois 60120, USA.

Printed in the United States of America

International Standard Book Number: 0-89191-488-9
Library of Congress Catalog Card Number: 81-66068

Designed by Rich Nickel

To my father-in-law, Daniel F. McPeak,
whose own pursuit of knowledge
gave him much understanding.

Contents

Acknowledgments

I am indebted to the many people who assisted me in completing the 1975 Papua New Guinea research project. A few of these people deserve special mention.

On research design and analysis: Rudolf Arnheim, Robert Caswell, Leonard W. Doob, Hall E. Duncan, Roy Gwyther-Jones, Kenneth Harwood, Sydney W. Head, John M. Kennedy, John M. Kittross, Abraham Ross, Henry Selby, Edward J. Trayes, and Anka Wagner. On assistance in the field: Richard Adler, Warren Croft, Ellis Deibler, Arturo B. Dominguez, Norbert Gondo (Maume), Dorothy James, Ambrosio G. Panugaling, Denise Potts, Dorothy Price, Ron and Margaret Reeson, Veda Rigden, Jesus and Nela Serrato, R. Daniel and Karen Shaw, Lahui Sipona, Robert Young, and my wife, Eileen Cook, who shared fully the burdens of this project. On development of this monograph: Charles T. Hein, Dennis Lowry, George McBean, Christopher H. Sterling, and Roland E. Wolseley.

Introduction

Academic literature suggests frequently that people in traditional areas of the world have trouble understanding pictures.[1] One example of a failure in understanding is documented by two Canadians, Abraham S. Ross, an anthropologist, and John M. Kennedy, a psychologist.[2] In 1974 they showed that older adults in New Guinea had difficulty recognizing pictures of objects—such as a fire—that have inherent movement.

Research I conducted a year later on the same island supported this finding. Two-thirds of the villagers interviewed often confused a drawing of a fire with other possibilities such as a flower, a fish, a leg, potatoes, spinach, a guitar, or a local container called a *sago* bag.

In another common perceptual failure, nonliterates in my study would identify a horizon line under a tree as the root of the tree or a vine. And one villager identified an outline picture of an airplane as a clothesline.

1. As used here, *traditional* refers to areas of the world that have been relatively isolated from Western culture. Many people in these areas are nonliterate (cannot and will not learn to read) or preliterate (cannot read but will learn).

2. John M. Kennedy and Abraham S. Ross, "Outline Picture Perception by the Songe of Papua," *Perception 4*, no. 4 (1975), pp. 391-406.

There has been a temptation to conclude from such perceptual problems that people in traditional areas lack ability to understand pictures. However, one has only to live among these people a short time to learn that their lower level of skill stems not from lack of ability, but from limited pictorial experience.

Development communicators are generally sensitive to this lack of pictorial experience.[3] Yet as one studies picture communication in traditional areas of the world, it becomes evident that pictures used in literacy primers, religious curriculum, posters, health manuals, and other printed materials, frequently interfere with messages intended to support development programs.

Several years ago, development communicators in Africa suggested to me that there was need for research that would help them use pictures more effectively in their work. The specific question they felt research could help them answer was, "What kinds of pictures communicate most effectively with people who have had little or no pictorial experience?"

This was the question I had in mind when in 1975, as part of a doctoral program in communication at Temple University, I spent five months in Papua New Guinea conducting field research in picture communication.

I hoped that my fieldwork would offer some useful conclusions about picture communication problems in this setting. For instance, I assumed it would be helpful to identify an art style that was both well liked and well understood by the people interviewed. More than that, I hoped that the project would suggest some new ideas about how development communicators could conduct research with a minimum of time and expense in the future.

But I'll never forget how George McBean, a UNICEF graphic artist, reacted the first time I presented the Papua New Guinea findings. The occasion was a 1979 Development Message Design Workshop at Stanford University. After I completed

---

3. Development communicators are publishers, artists, writers, literacy workers, and other message designers and media specialists who work in traditional areas like Papua New Guinea.

my presentation, McBean came up and said in effect, "Your research is like all the other research. It's fine, but little if any of it has produced any illustrations for the people who need them most."

Since that time, I have worked with McBean on the problem of extracting academic research from the ivory tower. In a very real sense, this monograph is a response to his challenge: to place research findings and principles into the hands of precisely those people who can make the most use of them.

The following pages present highlights of the research. Included are the research design, a brief summary of the interview, stimulus pictures, findings, and rules of thumb development communicators can adapt to their own areas of work.

In order to go beyond the 1975 study, practical methods for conducting research projects in the future are also suggested. In this way, development communicators can discover for themselves difficulties rural people are having in understanding pictures and determine what changes need to be implemented to make the pictures communicate more effectively.

The style and coverage here differ from standard academic practice. Any technical data is restricted to the notes or appendixes. In this way, it is hoped that those who care about using pictures effectively will grasp readily what I learned in Papua New Guinea and decide what it might mean for their work.

1 Setting for the Research

Papua New Guinea is a part of New Guinea, a large island that stretches 1,500 miles across the southwest Pacific, 100 miles off the northern tip of Australia. New Guinea is split by a national boundary: Irian Jaya, a part of Indonesia, is to the west, and independent Papua New Guinea, with its 1,000-mile chain of tropical islands is to the east.

Papua New Guinea itself is a land of blue-misted mountains, tropical forests, and lowland swamps. Wildlife includes snakes, lizards, crocodiles, and tortoises. In addition, there are birds of paradise as well as fruit-eating bats called flying foxes that have a wing span of up to three feet.

The people

Living in this smorgasbord of nature are three million people, of whom less than 30 percent have any formal education. They are divided into about 700 language areas, each of which has a distinct culture. Most of the 423 adult villagers interviewed for this project had traditional occupations such as caring for the garden, and building houses, fences, and bridges. Some said they were in religious or government work. There were nearly as many nonliterates as there were literates: only 49 percent of those interviewed passed the literacy test, and only 38 percent said they'd seen comic books. Many of the villagers contacted lived in such isolated areas they may have seen only a White Swan label on a can of tuna fish, a political party symbol, a photograph of a government leader, or an occasional magazine page affixed to a neighbor's grass hut.

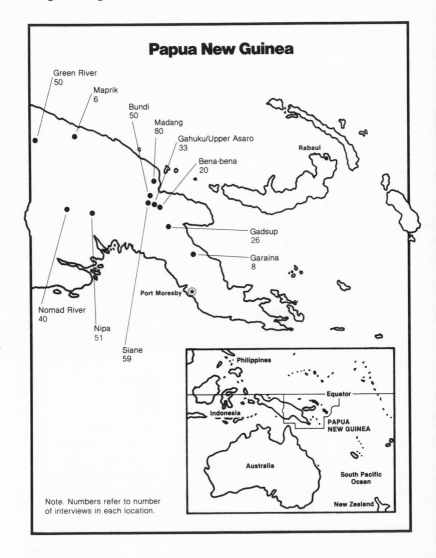

Papua New Guinea

Green River
50

Maprik
6

Bundi
50

Madang
80

Gahuku/Upper Asaro
33

Bena-bena
20

Rabaul

Gadsup
26

Garaina
8

Port Moresby

Nomad River
40

Nipa
51

Siane
59

Philippines

Equator

Indonesia

PAPUA
NEW GUINEA

Australia

South Pacific
Ocean

New Zealand

Note. Numbers refer to number
of interviews in each location.

Interview conditions

A summary of interview conditions is given in Table 1 on page 11. Pretest interviews were in controlled settings or comfortable environments: Baitabog Technical School (where students were eager to accept the snapshots of themselves offered), a Sepik River Area wood-carver's place of work, Riwo Village, and Siar Village, which was becoming a tourist attraction because of a recent visit from Queen Elizabeth of England.

Actual test interviews were usually held outside and in daylight on seats, which were loose tree stumps provided by the villagers. Responses were tallied on separate sheets of paper and inserted later into a loose-leaf notebook. Early interviews were recorded on a cassette recorder to compare varying uses of Melanesian Pidgin, for example, my own, with that of Norbert Maume Gondo, a young man from the highlands near Madang, who assisted with interviews in Madang and Bundi.

Each interview lasted 20-60 minutes, depending on translation requirements.[1] Two hundred seventy interviews were conducted in one language such as Melanesian Pidgin, Tokples, or English, while 153 involved a translator.

In the beginning, it was difficult to convince people to cooperate. Two work periods were lost, for example, when villagers who had gathered to rebuild a *sago* palm house and had plenty of time, still refused to be interviewed.

For many of these people, even speaking to a Westerner was a rare enough experience, much less having to complete such bizarre tasks as:

- recognizing a picture of a man drawn with a gap in the outline.
- picking one of two pictures that would complete a picture story.
- telling a story to go with a series of four pictures.
- deciding the sequence to use in reading a comic book.
- recognizing items in the series of pictures.

1. The time limit was imposed for personal reasons.

- estimating relative distance between items.
- picking out picture stories that had been seen five minutes earlier.

On many occasions, when an older man was approached for the interview, he would simply decline by lowering his head. Or when a woman was asked to participate, she would laugh self-consciously and run away. Eventually, we discovered that the women were more likely to participate when my wife, Eileen Cook, was doing the interviews. In fact, this is the reason that women figured as high as 41 percent in the total number of those interviewed.

The general problem of obtaining interviews was solved when David Bauli, a local schoolteacher, suggested that he set up morning appointments in various villages where people gathered as a group before going to work in the gardens.

A routine developed where the village elder would introduce us to the group, after which Norbert Gondo and I would explain that we needed help in developing better illustrations for local language versions of the Bible. The elder would then decide which villagers would do the interview.

This decision to dispense with random sampling and allow village elders to select subjects was a clear violation of Western research methods. However, given our experience on days when nobody would do the interviews, we decided it was better to accept direction because we were in no position to dictate terms. The only alternative would have been to spend a year in each village, which, of course, we couldn't do.

Another standard practice of Western research that became a quick casualty was conducting interviews in private. This was simply impossible. Though bystanders were asked to leave, they would grin, run away, and then sneak back and watch over our shoulders. As a result, lack of bystander control became one of the variables we had to contend with in the final analysis.

My theory was that preliterate people have no comprehension of what succeeding on a test means. Therefore, the thought of cheating or getting better grades never enters their minds. It seemed to me that in spying on the interview, subjects were merely showing interest in their enviable, collective way. When it came their turn to answer, they would respond straight from the heart, regardless of what they had seen before.

It was easy to determine when a day of interviews was completed. Someone would bring a coconut, slash a square hole in it with four strokes of a machete, and pass it around. In keeping with the culture, we would drink and then hand it to the next villager.

Table 1

Interview Conditions

Condition	Number of Interviews	Percent of total
Nonrandom sampling	All*	100%
Control of bystanders during interview		
Yes	174	41%
No	249	59%
Interviewer		
Researcher A	325	77%
Researcher B	94	22%
Other	4	1%
Language of interview		
Local language (tokples)	244	58%
Melanesian Pidgin	148	35%
Mixed	25	6%
English	6	1%
Number of steps in translation		
1 (English, Pidgin, and translations from local language to English)	270	64%
2 (Local languages translated into Pidgin)	153	36%

*Of these, 33 interviews were from a "census" sampling of Auya 2 village for which random sampling was artificially attempted during the evaluation of validity.

2   The Research Design

The first task in designing the research interview was to narrow the focus of the research, guided by the priorities of the local publishing situation. We knew from the start that we couldn't measure everything, and we didn't want to.

Our situation reminded me of a story from India about the monkey god, Hanuman, who flees from a terrific battle to fetch medication for a fierce warrior.[1] He reaches the mountain where the medication grows, but he is unable to identify which leaf he needs. Therefore, because he must hurry, and he cannot risk bringing back the wrong leaf, he brings the whole mountain to the battle.

That was one thing we could not do—bring the whole mountain of Western research to Papua New Guinea and try to incorporate it into one interview. At the same time, however, we wanted to bring enough of the mountain so that we would have relevant measures.

We began by eliminating many possible studies simply because they were impractical for our setting or biased in their

---

1. The story appears in *The Ramayana* of Hindu Vedic literature. See James A. Kirk, *Stories of the Hindus: An Introduction Through Text and Interpretation* (New York: Macmillan Co., 1972), pp. 208-209.

approach.[2]

Then we cataloged a number of variables that affect picture communication success. These were variables that related to the viewers and to the pictures. They are listed in Tables 2-4.

Table 2
Variables Related to Viewer's Skill

To determine how well viewer . . .

researchers can measure these skill indicators:

IDENTIFIES . . .

Recognition
Cue utilization
Closure
Verb choice
Passivity
Color discrimination
Global understanding (this
    item could fit under the
    other three skills as well)

ORGANIZES . . .

Spatial organization
Completion
Time relationships
    (sequencing)
Chaining

REMEMBERS . . .

Memory (remembering)

EVALUATES . . .

Preference
Interest
Attention
Literalness of interpretation
Impressionism

---

2. Some of the studies we avoided were: "black vs. white" studies (see page 105), studies of reactions to confusing optical illusions, studies of projected or electronically mediated pictures, studies requiring subjects to squint through an optical system and/or sit in a tilting wooden frame, and studies done in a Western setting or within schools of a traditional country.

Table 3
Variables Related to Viewer's Background and Experience

Variable Type	Variable Name
SOCIOLOGICAL	Age
	Sex of viewer
	Occupation
	Motivation of interest
	Religious affiliation
	Place (geographical location or language area)
	Distance from urban area
	Environment
	Mobility
EDUCATIONAL	Intelligence
	Experience with pictures
	Literacy (reading skill)
	Formal education (in years or by grade level)
	Education of instructors
	Education of parents

Table 4
Variables Related to Pictures

Variable Type	Variable Name
ORIGIN	Source
	Similarity to traditional art
CONTENT	Subject matter
	Background
	Realism (especially cultural accuracy, see also realism under *form,* below)
	Cultural accuracy
	Number of objects or actions (or centers of attention)
	Human figure representation
	Human figure posture
	Facial expression
	Implied motion
	Humor
	Vagueness

FORM	Realism (closely related to the next ten entries)
	Style (detail)
	Detail (style)
	Complexity
	Contrast
	Size (scale)
	Overlap
	Border cutoffs (where the picture's edge cuts off the image)
	Tone (shading)
	Shading (especially shadow areas)
	Color
	Picture series
	Split representation (depicting both sides at once, like a cutout showing a four-wheeled bicycle)
	Position on page
	Units of display (pages, frames)
	Medium (motion picture, television, slides, printed page)
	Combined factors
CONTEXT	Familiarity of object(s) to viewer(s)
	Relationship between art and text
	Functional relationship between publication and design and picture qualities
	Viewing context (group vs. individual)
	Perusal time

The next step was to determine primary areas of concentration in picture communication studies from around the world.[3] Using these past studies as a guide, we isolated ten variables from Table 2 that we felt would tell us whether art style was the most

3. We noted three primary areas of concentration: *(a)* the nature of perceptual failure in picture communication, such as seeing the picture too literally or focusing on parts before seeing the whole; *(b)* conditions that make perceptual failure more likely; and *(c)* how to prevent perceptual failure in unfavorable conditions.

important variable governing picture communication success and whether one art style worked best with the people interviewed. The ten variables were *closure, completion, verb choice, passivity, global understanding, chaining, sequencing, recognition, spatial organization,* and *remembering.* These ten variables, which became our key measures of picture understanding, are in the outline of the interview that follows.

In designing the interview, we felt it was important to add supplementary variables from Table 2 to act as backup measures. These are represented in steps 1, 2, 8, and 10 of the interview. Key sociological variables from Table 3—literacy, age, occupation, mobility, language, and experience with comic book pictures—are incorporated into steps 9 and 12. Variables from Table 4, which relate to the stimulus pictures themselves, are discussed in the following chapter.

The twelve steps of the interview, including definitions of the measures and how subjects scored, are discussed in detail in chapters 4 and 5.

The Research Interview

Step	Stimulus Materials	Sample Questions
1 Color preference	Chart with 14 color patches	"What color do you like best?"
2 Outline picture recognition *Closure*	Five randomly ordered outline pictures from 1975 Kennedy and Ross study	"What is this?" (repeated)
3 *Completion*	Five picture stories displayed on storyboards, randomly ordered by style and content.* The last frame of each story is omitted; subjects are given two extra pictures as options for the missing frames	"Which of the two pictures goes in the space without a picture here?"

*According to an experimental design worked out with Kennedy and Ross at the University of Toronto, each subject would see one set of pictures in each of the styles. The final decision was to use a quasi-experimental "counter-balanced" research design like that in Donald T. Campbell and Julian C. Stanley, *Experimental and Quasi-experimental Designs for Research* (Chicago: American Educational Research Association, 1963), pp. 50-52.

4 *Verb choice* *Passivity* *Global* *understanding* *Chaining*	The five completed picture stories from above, four frames apiece.	"The four pictures tell a story. Can you make a little story for each picture here?" (repeated for each of the five picture stories)
5 *Sequencing*	Same	"The four pictures tell a story. In this story, which picture do you think comes first? After that?" (repeated)
6 *Recognition*	Same	"What is this?" (repeated for different details in the pictures)
7 *Spatial organization*	Same	"In which picture do you think the _____ is close to (far from) the _____. (repeated)
8 Style preference	Randomly ordered display of the fourth frame from each picture story (In this way all five art styles are seen.)	"Which picture do you like best? After that?" (repeated)
9 Literacy	Cover of Kristen Pres literacy primer with title: *Nau Yu Ken Rit na Rait.* (Melanesian Pidgin for "Now You Can Read and Write." In some cases a local language was used.)	"Can you read this?" (If subject could not, the stimulus was quickly withdrawn.)

10 Verbal story completion	Verbal story. (The story is printed on page 69.)	After the story is read, the following is said, "The story is finished now. Which of these two statements about the story is right? The man dies and his head comes up a coconut. Or, the children play marbles." (alternate these)
11 *Remembering*	Ten picture stories, four frames apiece. Five of the stories have been seen before, five have not.	"Now I have ten pictures to show. Some pictures I showed you before and some pictures I did not. If you think I showed you a picture before, say, 'Yes, I see.' If you think I did not show you this picture, say, 'No.' "
12 Age	None	"After which war were you born?"
Geographic and language area		"Where are you from?"
Occupation		"What is your work?"
Mobility		"On what day did you go to _____?" (city or government post)
Comic book experience		"Have you read comic books or or not?"

3   The Pictures

As the components of a research interview are assembled, key decisions have to be made about what kinds of pictures to test. (See variables related to pictures in Table 4 on page 15.)

Research literature suggests that artists should use realistic pictures when working in traditional areas like Papua New Guinea.[1] The problem with this guideline is that the exact nature of realistic pictures is never defined.

In practice, realistic means culturally accurate detailed line drawings with natural proportions and, if applicable, natural color (see page 84). But then the question comes up, is this view of realism (accuracy and natural proportion) valid for every culture? Or, to ask another question, is realism a matter of content and cultural relevance at all? Some studies suggest it has more to do with style.[2]

---

1. For a few of the many examples of how the standard dictum, "be realistic," is used and applied to research and illustrations, see the following studies: Seth Joseph Spaulding, "An Investigation of Factors Which Influence the Effectiveness of Fundamental-Education Reading Materials for Latin-American Adults" (Ph.D. diss., Ohio State University, 1953), pp. 146, 245; Jan Thomaeus, "Training Book Illustrators in South Asia," *Fundamental and Adult Education* 10, no. 4 (October 1958), pp. 163-167; Charles Granston Richards, ed. and comp., *The Provision of Popular Reading Materials,* pp. 257-260, 265-267, 269.

2. For example, see Anne Zimmer and Fred Zimmer, *Visual Literacy in Communication,* p. 57.

Style

The way we approached the issue was simply to test five different art styles and try to determine how each style affected picture communication. The questions we tried to answer were: Would art style be the most important variable governing picture communication success? And, which art style would work best?

The five art styles chosen represented typical options development communicators in Papua New Guinea have in choosing art:

The five art styles

1. **Stick figure drawings.**
2. **Faceless outline drawings like those Annie Vallotton used in the Good News Bible (Today's English Version).**
3. **Detailed black-and-white drawings.**
4. **Detailed drawings with color.**
5. **Black-and-white photographs.**

Content

Five different story contents were developed to go along with the five art styles. In this way, it was possible to compare whether art style affected understanding scores more than story content.

All in all, not counting the pictures we borrowed from Kennedy and Ross, the basic stimulus set consisted of 25 pictures: five different stories made in each of five different styles. They are reprinted on pages 24-48 according to the order in which they were tested. These particular stories were chosen because, in pretesting, they were well understood and seemed relevant to both highland and lowland areas of Papua New Guinea.

The fact that the stories were culturally relevant raised as many questions as it answered. For one thing, it did not permit a test of cultural relevance as a factor in picture understanding. (We had no culturally irrelevant pictures as a basis for comparison.) Furthermore, by choosing content that was familiar to the people, we were minimizing the chances for the very perceptual failures we were trying to measure. Thus, our approach was a far cry from classical research, which, in order to maintain a bell-shaped curve, increases the chances of failure by choosing content that is foreign to its viewers.[3]

Preparing the pictures

Rough sketches for four story pictures were prepared by Roy E. Gwyther-Jones, an Australian artist in Manila, Philippines, who had worked for years in Papua New Guinea. Final story-boards and color overlays were completed by Arturo B. Dominguez, a commercial artist who was specializing in popular comic books in the Philippines. In Papua New Guinea, Lahui Sipona, the staff artist at Kristen Pres, a local publishing house, corrected the Manila art for cultural detail and prepared new color overlays as the ones from Manila could not be used. We chose to use only three of the original story pictures; two of the stories in the final set of five were his own (a woman fetching bananas and a man building a *kunai* grass hut). All photographs were taken locally.

Though the research did include some imported art, final decisions on all artwork and photography were left to Lahui Sipona. While it would have been possible to exert greater control of the art quality through perceptual analysis and criticism, this process would have biased the art with Western preconceptions.[4] On the other hand, the lack of criticism involved the risk that the final product might be something less than ideal.

This is, in fact, what happened. Photographs, for example, were generally fuzzy because the paper used for printing was too absorbent. Not only that, the artist made the decision to keep the background of each photograph in focus when putting the

---

3. This content dilemma was just one of the conflicts we experienced in trying to apply Western research methods to Papua New Guinea. In many areas, almost without being aware of it, we turned our backs on the canons of Western research methodology. Later on, when we returned to the academic community, the chill winds of critical analysis told us how very complex cross-cultural research can be.

4. Naturally, we worked closely with Sipona and, in fact, as much as possible, he incorporated principles of effective picturing previous research studies had uncovered. (These principles are listed on page 84.)

backgrounds out of focus would have highlighted the central figure.[5]

The stick figures and outline pictures also had numerous problems. Some could be seen as puppets or monsters, and often there were confusing details in the background.

The following stick figure frame from the woodcutter story serves as an example:

5. Sipona argued that viewers would prefer a natural background rather than one which was out of focus. He felt that John Sievert's earlier Papua New Guinea research on style had erred in making drawings to match photographs. He resolved to do the opposite in our study and match the photographs with the artwork he'd already completed. In retrospect, it turned out that each medium, drawing and photography, was so unique that neither one could be made to match the other in a test of this sort.

The human figure and the tree seem to float above the frame boundary. This distraction is compounded by the fact that the branches of the tree disappear at the top into jagged lines that only suggest the leaves that one would expect to see. As for the man, he seems to be aiming his ax at a point far above the portion of the tree that has been cut. In addition, the ax handle visually coincides with his arms, and it looks like it is growing out of his head. In a way, too, the ax looks almost as if it is aimed at the man's head.

Printing of the pictures was done on a small Rotoprint offset press by the Anglican Centre in Madang at the cost of $575.94 (U.S. dollars).[6] The plan was to print enough copies so that each subject interviewed could respond to a clean copy of the pictures. At the last minute, however, a scheduling problem at the press made it impossible for them to do the color printing. Color was added by painting in with watercolor wash. It was feared that the single copy would become soiled quickly, but it turned out the color pictures remained clean and intact throughout the months of interviewing.

The five picture stories

Following are the five picture stories that formed the basis of the research interview. Each story is printed in the five art styles.

6. Considering costs of artwork, materials, platemaking, and printing, the production cost was $3.06 per interview. Reproduction for further testing and distribution, based upon the 1975 Anglican Centre figures, at a quantity of 423 copies, would have been $1.36 per interview.

PICTURE STORY ①
A man chopping wood

A. Stick figure drawing

 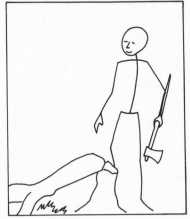

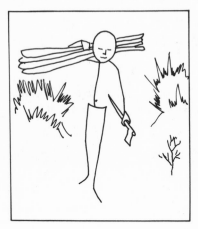 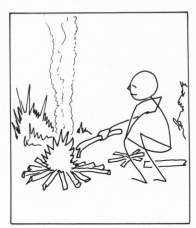

B. Faceless outline drawing (like those used in Good News Bible)

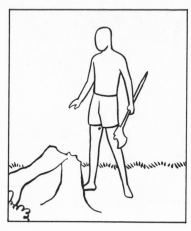

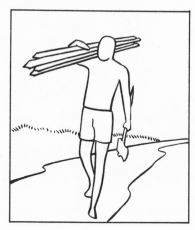

C. Detailed black-and-white drawing

D. Detailed black-and-white drawing with watercolor wash (the color can only be suggested here)

E. Black-and-white photographs

PICTURE STORY 2
A woman fetching bananas

A. Stick figure drawing

B. Faceless outline drawing

C. Detailed black-and-white drawing

D. Detailed black-and-white drawing with watercolor wash

E. Black-and-white photographs

PICTURE STORY 3
A woman growing and fetching corn

A. Stick figure drawing

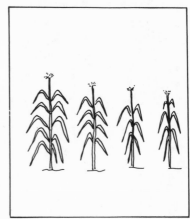

B. Faceless outline drawing

C. Detailed black-and-white drawing

D. Detailed black-and-white drawing with watercolor wash

E. Black-and-white photographs

PICTURE STORY 4
A man building a *kunai* grass hut

A. Stick figure drawing

B. Faceless outline drawing

C. Detailed black-and-white drawing

D. Detailed black-and-white drawing with watercolor wash

E. Black-and-white photographs

PICTURE STORY 5
A man killing a pig

A. Stick figure drawing

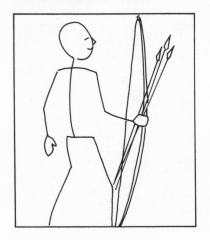

B. Faceless outline drawing

C. Detailed black-and-white drawing

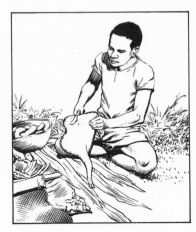

D. Detailed black-and-white drawing with watercolor wash

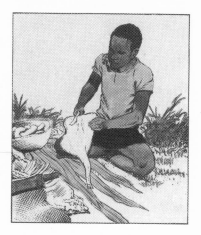

E. Black-and-white photographs

4   The Interview: Steps 1-7

Chapters 4 and 5 describe the 12 steps of the research interview. Included are brief summaries of each task, definitions of the measures, and summaries of the scores. The key measures of picture understanding are printed in italic.

Step 1 Color preference

The interview opened with a color-preference test. A color chart of 14 colors was displayed, and the following question was asked: "Which color do you like best?"[1] If further explanation was needed, we noted that our purpose was to discover which color to use for book covers, particularly the Bible.

Results. Dark blue was the favorite color in this limited test, followed by red, light green, yellow, and dark green. About two-thirds (68 percent) of those who chose dark blue were literate. Nonliterates showed a slightly greater preference for red (18 percent of the nonliterates chose red; 14 percent of them chose dark blue). Subjects who chose dark blue could have been influenced by mention of Bible covers, as the Melanesian Pidgin New Testament in Papua New Guinea has a dark blue cover.

---

1. The 14 colors were light green, dark green, orange, yellow, aqua blue, dark brown, red, light brown, dark blue, dark orange, magenta, grey, maroon, and light magenta.

Step 2a Outline picture recognition

   Outline picture recognition measured subjects' skill at recognizing outline figures in pictures.[2] Subjects were asked to identify wholes and parts of five randomly ordered outline figures taken from a study developed earlier by Kennedy and Ross for the Songe people of Papua New Guinea.[3] (Four of the figures are reprinted here; the fifth figure is discussed in step 2b.) One point was scored for each correct answer in response to the questions, "What is this? Where is its _____ (tail, leg, ear)?"

2. This variable was included as a backup measure to validate recognition in step 6.

3. Kennedy and Ross, "Outline Picture Perception," *Perception* 4, no. 4 (1975), pp. 394-396.

Results. For this recognition test, 72 percent of the respon-
dents had perfect scores. The picture that caused the most trouble
was the tree for which only 38 percent had a perfect score. The
results generally confirmed Kennedy and Ross's earlier finding
that Papua New Guinea villagers can recognize these pictures
without difficulty. See Appendix 2, page 101.

Step 2b *Closure*

One of the recognition tasks from Kennedy and Ross involved *closure*, the first of the ten key measures of picture understanding.[4] Closure measured skill at recognizing a picture having incomplete boundary lines. Following the example of Kennedy and Ross, we covered all the figures below except for the one on the far left.

If subjects recognized this outline figure, which is the most incomplete one, they received a perfect score of 5. Points were lost as subjects needed to see more and more of the figure in order to recognize it. The test was helpful in determining subjects' skill at mentally connecting discontinuous lines and grasping structural concepts from incomplete stimuli.[5]

4. Kennedy and Ross, "Outline Picture Perception," p. 394.

5. Theoretically, of course, all pictures are incomplete representations when you compare them with the real object.

Results. All but 100 of the subjects scored a perfect 5 because they could recognize the most incomplete figure. The task was difficult for persons living in areas having less contact with Western culture (Green River and Nomad River areas) and for marginally literate or nonliterate people.

Step 3 *Completion*

The next task involved *completion,* a measure of skill at choosing the correct final frame to complete a picture series.

The five picture stories were displayed in random order according to style and content.[6] In each case, the last frame of the story was omitted as in the following example:

6. The pictures were randomly ordered according to the results of a monotonous coin-tossing session one weekend. Thus, the test was only as random as the coins.

For the five stories, subjects were asked to choose the correct final picture from two options. The following two options, for example, were given for the picture story above:

Since the picture on the right depicts a man cutting meat, it represents the correct final choice for the pig hunt sequence.

Like the closure measure, completion gave an idea of the subjects' cognitive skill in grasping structural concepts from incomplete stimuli.[7] Subjects were given a passing or failing score depending on whether they successfully completed the story.

Results. It became clear during analysis that scores tended to improve as subjects performed tasks over and over for the five picture stories. Since this improvement could indicate that subjects understood the tasks better later in the interview, it was decided to restrict the final analysis to the last story for each interview.[8] This was done not only for this task, but for the tasks in steps 2-7 as well.

The average completion score for all subjects on the last picture story was .72 out of a possible 1. It was found that for all

7. The two measures differ in that closure only requires skill in perceiving pictorial space while completion requires the additional skill of discerning time sequence for pictures in series.

8. This decision led to unequal numbers of subjects' seeing pictures according to each content and style. For example, 92 subjects saw the woodcutter story in last position, 78, the banana story, 88, the corn story, 84, the *kunai* house story, and 81, the pig story.

styles and stories, the people who had the most trouble in completion were from the Nomad River, Nipa, and Green River areas, all of which had had very little contact with the West. Photographs did slightly better in all areas. People seemed to be able to match the pictures better for photographs because they could recognize the faces.

Step 4 Open-ended story (containing four measures: *verb choice, passivity, global understanding,* and *chaining*)

For the open-ended story, the five picture stories were displayed in random order according to style and content. Subjects were asked to "tell a little story for each picture here" and describe what they thought was going on in each picture in any order they chose.

For example, when shown the building of a *kunai* grass hut story,

one 38-year-old man from the Auya 2 village responded as follows:

Frame Number (order in which subject described frames)	Response
3	"Man* he is holding the *morata*" (a roof thatch).
1	"Man* he is holding the *şapnit*" (sewn *sago* leaves).
2	"Man* he is holding the *pangal" (sago* palm stalks used in walls of local houses).
4	"He, too." (The verb holding is implied.)

The open-ended story was versatile in that it provided four measures: *verb choice, passivity, global understanding,* and *chaining.* As indicated in step 2, only scores from the last picture story in each interview were used in the final analysis.

---

*Asterisks signify that the subject stopped repeatedly at the single word *man* in response to the request that he tell a story for each picture. In each case, he had to be prodded further before he would elaborate.

Verb choice measured the correctness of the verbs used by subjects in telling stories from the pictures. One point was assigned for each frame that elicited a correct verb. For example, in frame 4 where the man is taking the palm stalks to the house, correct verbs might be "carrying" or "building" while incorrect verbs would be "sitting" or "sewing." The Auya 2 villager cited had a perfect score of 4, as he used a correct verb, "holding," for each of the four frames.

Results for verb choice. The average score for all 423 subjects was 3.78 out of a possible 4. Obviously, the score would have been lower if content less compatible with the culture had been chosen for the pictures.

Passivity measured lack of involvement or interest in the picture stories as reflected by the use of passive verbs (being, having, holding, sitting, standing) in the open-ended story response.[9] One point was assigned for each picture-story frame in which a passive verb was used. In the example above about building the *kunai* grass hut, the Auya 2 villager scored 4, as he had used or implied the passive verb "holding" for each frame.[10]

Results for passivity. On a 0-4 range, with 4 the highest, the average score of the subjects was .92. Higher scores on this measure—indicating increased use of passive verbs—occurred among older people, nonliterates, marginal literates, people who had not seen comic books before the test, and for 20 people who had not visited a city or government post for 61-180 days. Such a tendency may have indicated these subjects were less interested in the test or more easily distracted from it.

Global understanding was a subjective evaluation of how well subjects understood the concepts of the picture stories. A

9. See Rudolf Arnheim, *Visual Thinking*, p. 67; Bernard Shaw, *Visual Symbols Survey*, p. 39.

10. Note the similarity between passivity and verb choice. The difference is that verb choice evaluates correctness, and passivity reflects interest. For example, "holding" the *sapnit* was correct for frame 1 of the series about building the *kunai* grass hut, but an active verb like "pulling" the *sapnit* would have shown more interest in the action depicted.

subject who recognized the four major events in the story sequence earned 4 points. Points were deducted as subjects failed to understand one, two, or even more major concepts in the stories.

Results for global understanding. On a scale of 0-4 with 4 the highest, subjects scored an average of 3.07. Older, more traditional people had lower scores. Higher scores occurred for younger people or for people who had experience with literacy training or comic books. These findings suggest that understanding of pictures increases with experience. Often it is the younger people who have broader experience with other cultures. For example, in some areas, Bundi for instance, a young man is expected to spend a year wandering from place to place after he is betrothed. Of course, the subjectivity of these scores should not be ignored.

Chaining measured tendency to refer to more than one frame at a time in telling a story, thereby integrating the story's actions.[11] One point was assigned for each frame that elicited reference to action in another frame of the story. For example, in the woman-fetching-bananas story, for the statement, "Having gathered the bananas" (third frame),

---

11. This is not the same chaining used in behavioral psychology.

"the woman then carried them home" (fourth frame),

the subject would receive 1 point.

Results for chaining. Chaining occurred rarely in the interviews. On a scale of 0-4 with 4 the highest, the average score was .43.

Occasionally, in the pig hunt sequence, subjects commented that the man pictured in one frame might shoot the man pictured in the adjacent frame:

In other words, instead of seeing the series as the same man in four sequential poses, they saw it as four different men performing the actions in all the frames at the same time—as if the subjects were watching through a window that had four panes of glass separated by bars. This tendency was termed *framing*, and it could have been significant, but only 31 out of 423 subjects demonstrated it.

Step 5 *Sequencing*

Sequencing measured skill at pointing to the correct chronological order for reading the pictures. Subjects were asked to point out the order in which the four frames in each of the five picture stories should be viewed. A score of 3 points was assigned for western sequencing (left-to-right, top-to-bottom); 2 points for clockwise; 1 point for counterclockwise, and 0 points if no system was used.[12]

Results. Out of a possible 3 points, subjects scored an average of 1.70. Again, scores were lower for people who had less contact with Western culture. This particular finding suggests that the Western left-to-right, top-to-bottom eye movement in a picture series is a learned convention. Further analysis showed that for those who had not yet learned to read, only 17 percent used Western sequencing, while 30 percent went clockwise and 23 percent went counterclockwise.

The tendency to go in a circle makes sense, as a circular path is actually more natural than a trace-retrace system. Even a boustrophedon zigzag system like an ox uses when plowing a field (left-to-right, then down and right-to-left) would be more natural than Western sequencing.

Step 6 *Recognition*

Recognition measured skill at identifying objects in pictures. Subjects were asked to name four items in each picture story. One point was assigned for each correct item named

---

12. A non-Western sequence could make sense in some cases. For example, in the chopping-wood story, the sequence could go counterclockwise from frame 4 by having the man make a fire, then bring additional wood, and then go out and cut some more.

(usually a large and a small item in each of the right-hand frames).[13]

Results. Out of a possible 4 points, subjects scored 3.41 on the average. Again, older and more traditional villagers scored lower. These findings confirmed our analysis from global understanding that picture understanding increases with experience. The results also imply that though older people have been around longer, they still have less experience with pictures than younger people.

There were two other important findings related to recognition. First, the subjects recognized human figures more easily than other objects. The success rate for recognizing human figures was 97 percent compared to 96 percent for tools and weapons, 89 percent for things in the environment, 94 percent for partial figures, 77 percent for objects on the ground, 67 percent for fire, and only 37 percent for the horizon line under a tree.

Second, subjects had difficulty recognizing single-frame scenes depicting the passing of time. Take, for example, the series showing the woman growing corn:

13. Every effort was made to judge responses within the cultural context of Papua New Guinea. For example, if a subject called a tree "firewood," a correct score was assigned as this answer reflected common usage in Melanesian Pidgin.

The second frame is supposed to be portraying corn in the process of growing, however, many subjects stalled and could not think of a proper verb. Many of them simply said, "corn," and their score fell by one point.

The implication is that for preliterate people, a single picture is not enough to show that time is passing. In the above example, it might have helped to show the woman tilling the earth, sowing the seeds, covering the seeds, weeding the garden, and then admiring her knee-high stalks.

Step 7 *Spatial organization*

Spatial organization measured skill at recognizing space relationships within pictures (how far items were from each other).

For this task, only the pig hunt sequence was used. Subjects were asked the following two questions: "In which picture do you think the _____ (name item) is *close* to _____ ?" "In which picture do you think the _____ is *far* from the _____ ?" For both of these questions, the same two items would be referred to. A passing score of 1 point was given for choosing the correct frame(s) in answer to the questions. (A response was considered correct if either or both questions were answered correctly.)

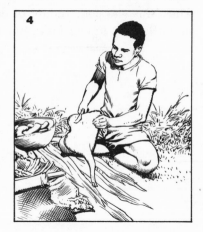

Results. Subjects averaged .89 points out of a possible perfect score of 1. Only 46 people missed the question. This high performance rate conflicts with a number of research studies on pictorial depth perception, especially in Africa.[14] Based on our experience in Papua New Guinea, I would say that subjects in the

14. Many of these studies repeatedly demonstrated European superiority in detecting depth relationships in outline pictures. See especially William Hudson's article, "Pictorial Depth Perception in Subcultural Groups in Africa," *The Journal of Social Psychology* 52, no. 2 (1960), pp. 183-208.

African studies scored low because they were misinterpreting the terms *close* and *far*. [15]

This is what happened in our own study. When asked in which frame the arrow was closest to the pig, for example, one man from the village of Yabob answered by pointing to the second frame of the series.

The arrow is *far away* in distance, but is *close* in terms of how soon it will pierce the pig and how accurately the hunter is aiming. The same villager then went on to point out that in frame 1, he thought the arrow was far from the pig.

When responses like this occurred, we tried to probe more deeply by asking whether the arrow had ''got'' the pig or not. This respondent was one of the 26 subjects who said the arrow was closest to the pig in frame 2, but that it had not yet hit the pig. Thus, this was not a failure of perception as the African studies might lead us to conclude, but rather a question of semantics.

15. Although William Hudson's 1960 study denies this problem, the first study of pictorial depth perception acknowledges that the words *close* and *far* contributed to misunderstanding. See W. H. R. Rivers, ''Vision,'' *Physiology and Psychology*, vol. 3, *Reports of the Cambridge Anthropological Expedition to the Torres Straits*, ed. A. C. Haddon (London: Cambridge University Press, 1901), pp. 97-98.

5

The Interview: Steps 8-12

Chapter 4 covers steps 8-12 in the step-by-step outline of the research interview.

Step 8 Style preference

To evaluate style preference, or the subjects' favorite art style, all five art styles were displayed in random order:

Detailed black-and-white drawing

Stick figure

Detailed black-and-white with color

Photograph

Faceless outline drawing

As shown here, the five art styles were represented by the fourth frame of the same picture story. The picture story used for the task was changed from interview to interview.

Subjects were asked this series of questions: "Which picture do you like best? After that? After that?" In addition to first choice, second, third, fourth, and last choices were tabulated in order to validate first choices as well as all styles together. Lahui Sipona, the artist, had suggested that we ask why subjects preferred a particular style, but this question was deleted later because answers were either noncommittal ("I'm not sure.") or indicated that subjects felt they'd made a mistake. Some tried to correct the answer they'd just given, and a few stared at the ground in silence.

Results. The major finding here was that art style did have a distinct effect on subjects' preference for pictures. Their first choice was color, and the second choice was split between the black-and-white drawings and the photographs. (Photographs may have fared better if they had been higher quality. Of course that would have applied to any of the other styles as well.)

Less liked were the outline pictures that lacked facial details, and least liked were the stick figures. It is worth noting, too, that what the people liked best wasn't necessarily what they understood best. Color, which nonliterate people chose above all others, actually distracted them from describing actions in the stories.

Step 9 Literacy[1]

In defining literacy, the late Sarah Gudschinsky, literacy coordinator for Summer Institute of Linguistics, Inc., stated "a person is literate who, in a language that he speaks, can read and understand anything that he would have understood if it had been spoken to him; and who can write, so that it can be read, anything that he can say."[2] Persons failing to satisfy these conditions are said to be preliterate or nonliterate. (The word illiterate is avoided as it has a pejorative connotation.)

To test subjects' literacy, we asked them to read aloud the following title from the literacy primer cover from Kristen Pres (Melanesian Pidgin spelling for Christian Press):

Nau You Ken Rit na Rait (Now You Can Read and Write)[3]

1. Literacy was used to help evaluate formal education, a difficult variable to measure because educational techniques vary widely from place to place. Analyzing formal education in each study area would have been a research project in itself.

2. Sarah C. Gudschinsky, *A Manual of Literacy for Preliterate Peoples,* ed. Ramona Lucht, Jacqueline Firechow, and Eunice Loeweke (Ukarumpa, Papua New Guinea: Summer Institute of Linguistics, 1973), p. 5.

3. Wesley Sadler, *Nau yu Ken Rit na Rait* (Madang, Papua New Guinea: Kristen Pres, 1972).

In interviews where Melanesian Pidgin was not spoken, a local language equivalent for this expression was used.[4]

The literacy test demanded sensitivity. If subjects clearly could not read the title or acted embarrassed, the stimulus was quickly withdrawn, and the next task was presented. A passing score of 1 point was given for reading the title correctly.

Results. Scores for three of the subjects were lost, but of those subjects recorded, 49 percent were literate, and 49 percent could not read (figures rounded off). Seven subjects read with such difficulty they were coded as marginally literate. These were grouped with the literate subjects for the final analysis. Generally, it was difficult to separate literacy and local cultural effects on picture understanding. The reason for this was simply that the cultural areas where people scored highest in the interview were the same areas where people had learned to read. And the cultural areas where people scored lower were the same areas where people were just being introduced to literacy training.

Step 10 Verbal story completion

In the next step, a local folktale about how the first coconut came to Papua New Guinea was read aloud. Our assistant, Norbert Gondo, had adapted the tale from a local writer's magazine.

Ellis Deibler, translator for Summer Institute of Linguistics in the Gahuku area, had demonstrated for us how stories were told in Papua New Guinea culture. We were to employ forceful gestures and a great variety of inflection in our voices, punctuated by sibilant breathing and other vocal sound effects.

We introduced the story with these words: "I will read you a little story. After this story, I have two statements about the story. One statement is right, and the other is no good. Now, it is up to you to find which statement is right. The story starts now."

And then we told the story.

---

4. Area languages were translated by specialists who worked with the Summer Institute of Linguistics in Ukarumpa. They had all lived in these areas for extended periods of time.

Men from one place go to an island to hunt birds. In the morning they get their canoes and go to this island. After coming to the island they go into the bush. They kill many birds now and they go back, but they leave one man behind. The man comes back and sees the canoes are not there. He shouts, but the men have gone. He gets a tree from the beach and swims away. But the shark eats him and his head floats home on the water. His wife finds his head in the morning and buries it near his house. After a while something comes up bearing fruit. The woman gets one and drinks its juice and it is very sweet. She takes it to everyone and they throw some in the sea and they go to places all around.[5]

After the story was told, subjects were asked to choose which of the following statements was correct, or if that was confusing, which of the statements best summarized the story:

- *The man dies and his head comes up a coconut.*

- *The children play marbles.*

The statements were interchanged for different interviews. A passing score of 1 point was given for choosing the correct statement about the story. In this way we tabulated scores for verbal story completion, which, like closure and completion, measured cognitive skill in grasping a concept and supplying missing information. The difference here was that the stimulus was verbal.

In addition to giving us a measure of verbal story completion, the story helped to make the interview more interesting and compatible with the culture. The sessions were most relaxed and spontaneous during the telling of the story. Furthermore, the story put more time between the first showing of the picture stories and the memory test in step 11.

5. Opunai Hosea, "Pes Kokonas," *Papua New Guinea Writing*, no. 15 (1974), pp. 20-21.

Results. Our intention was to use responses to compare verbal versus picture story completion skill. We determined, however, that when subjects failed, it was because the story had been told too quickly. Therefore, this measure could not be used in further analysis.

Step 11 *Remembering*

Remembering measured skill in recognizing pictures seen during an earlier part of the interview.

Ten picture stories were displayed randomly according to content and style. Five of the stories were the ones seen previously, and five were new. The five new stories were prepared in the same five art styles as the basic sets:

New stories for memory test

How to make a canoe

The government agent brings a road to the village

From craftmanship to purchasing power

Treating malaria at the clinic

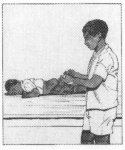

Selling vegetables at the market

As the pictures were presented, we said, "Now I have ten pictures to show you. Some pictures I showed you before and some pictures I did not show you before. If you think I showed this picture before, say, 'Yes, I see.' If you think I did not show you this picture, say, 'No.' Do you think I showed you this picture, or not?'' (Indicate picture.)

A passing score of 1 point was given if subjects correctly identified the picture story seen earlier. An additional content memory variable was coded if the subject correctly recognized that he had *not* seen a new picture.

Results. Only 17 out of 423 subjects missed the test for remembering. This high performance level on memory for pictures is consistent with much of the psychological literature on recognition.

Step 12 Sociological variables

At the end of the interview, the standard questions on age, geographic/language area, and occupation were asked. One school of research argues that these questions should be asked first. The second school of thought, which we followed, argues that it is better to ask them last because they could be threatening questions, and, as the theory goes, it is better not to intimidate subjects at the start. Another reason to ask them last is that it places priority on the picture communication questions.

Since many subjects did not know their exact age, we obtained a rough estimate by asking such questions as "After which war were you born?'' Or, "How big were you when the war started?''

For geographic/language area, we simply asked, "Where are you from?''

The occupation question was asked mainly to distinguish between traditional and nontraditional occupations. Traditional occupations included working the garden, hunting, or building fences, bridges, or houses. Nontraditional occupations included work related to religion, government, transportation, retail sales, medical or translation assistance, mining, labor, education, and a few other specialties.

The question for occupation was, "What is your work while you are here?" We sometimes elaborated by saying, "Do you work in the garden, or break up firewood, or what?"

Other sociological variables related to mobility (how long it had been since subjects had traveled to a city) and to comic book experience. For mobility, we asked, "On what day did you go to _____ ?" For comic book experience, we asked, "Have you read comic books or not?" If subjects acted confused, we explained that comic books were picture books showing cowboys or soldiers. (According to my assistant, Gondo, most local comics were about warfare.)

If subjects responded "Yes," to our questions about comic books in a fairly remote area, we asked, "Where did you see the comic books?" On occasion, subjects would say that they had seen comic books, but had not read them. This suggested they held comic books in low regard or felt that we might. This response occurred so infrequently, however, the generalization was not confirmed.

The sociological variables are summarized in Table 5.

Table 5
Description of Villagers Interviewed

Characteristic	Number	Percent
Sex of Subject		
Male	250	59%
Female	173	41%
Age		
13-34	267	63%
35-56	131	31%
57-78	25	6%
Literacy Skill (from step 9) [a]		
Literate	207	49%
Nonliterate	206	49%
Marginally literate	7	2%
Not known	3	1%

a. It was not intentional that there would be a nearly equal number of literates and nonliterates in the sample.

Language Area [b]

Bel, Amele	79	19%
Gadsup	26	6%
Gende, Siane, Asaro, Gahuku, Bena bena, and Angal Heneng	213	50%
Yuri	50	12%
Samo, Kubo	40	9%
Ambulas	6	1%
Guhu Samane	8	2%
A visitor (origin unknown)	1	0%

Occupation

Traditional (such as farming)	304	72%
Religious	46	11%
Government	18	4%
Other (nontraditional)	51	12%
Unknown	4	1%

Number of days since last visit to city or nearby government post

0-30 days	374	88%
31-180 days	26	6%
More than 180 days	23	5%

Comic book experience

Yes	161	38%
No	257	61%
No answer	5	1%

b. The larger language areas are formally named as follows: Madang- Adelbert Range Sub-Phylum (including Bel or Gedaged and Amele), East Central Trans-New Guinea Phylum (in which the East New Guinea Highlands Stock includes Gadsup, and the East Central Family includes Gende, Siane, Asaro, Gahuku, Bena bena, and Angal Heneng), Sepik Geographic Region (including Yuri, an unclassified area called Karkar—not the island—by local missionaries), and Trans-New Guinea Phylum, East Strickland Family (including Samo and Kubo dialect areas among the Nomad languages).

Quality of the findings[6]

The methodology of our Papua New Guinea study was explicit enough to consider the validity and reliability of the findings.

Through an elaborate series of tests, it was possible to determine that the findings were basically sound. Nonrandom sample selection, allowing bystanders to watch the interview, using more than one interviewer and more than one language were all examined as possible sources of invalidity. It was found, however, that in each case, for various reasons the measures remained valid.[7]

Furthermore, when the ten measures were double-checked by comparing them with criterion or related measures, all of the measures except remembering passed the test.[8] When the scores of the measures were tested for stability and internal consistency the conclusion was that they were all reliable except for two, completion and spatial organization.

A recheck of all scores revealed an error of only 2 percent in coding. Of these errors, 47 percent were due to changes in procedure during the coding process, 24 percent were differences in subjective judgment, 3 percent were errors in punch-card preparation, and the rest were unclassified. These errors were corrected before doing the final analysis.

6. For further information on evaluating the quality of research findings, see the following studies on validity and reliability: Robert L. Thorndike, ed., *Educational Measurement*, 2nd ed. (Washington, D.C.: American Council on Education, 1971), pp. 356-507; Ernest R. House, *Evaluating with Validity* (Beverly Hills, California: Sage Publications, Inc., 1980).

7. For example, when scores for early interviews were compared with scores for later interviews in five villages where bystanders had not been controlled, it was found that only one measure in ten (sequencing) showed a significant difference. Not only that, but scores from later interviews were actually *lower* than scores for earlier interviews.

8. Remembering had so many passing scores, an evaluation of validity here could have been misleading.

Conclusions

Was picture understanding affected more by sociological factors, or by content and style? We obtained the answer by determining how significantly each of the key ten measures of picture understanding had been affected by style and content and by the various sociological variables: sex of subject, age, literacy, language area, occupation, mobility, and comic book experience.[9] After analyzing the effect in each case, we came up with the following conclusions.

First of all, our hypothesis that art style would have the greatest influence on picture understanding was not supported by the findings. In fact, art style had a significant effect on only four of the key measures of picture understanding. Language area and literacy each affected nine measures; occupation and age each affected seven; comic book experience and content each affected six of the key measures. Scores for the measures affected were consistently lower in the three language areas where people had had least contact with literacy training and western culture: Nipa, Nomad River, and Green River.

Only sex of subject and mobility affected fewer of the key measures than did art style. Sex of subject affected only one measure. Men had higher scores for chaining (seeing relationships between pictures). This was probably because it is the men in Papua New Guinea culture who sit around the fire and tell stories and are therefore the more sophisticated storytellers. Mobility had no significant effect at all on the measures.

These results demonstrated without a doubt that environmental factors such as language area, literacy training, occupation, and comic book experience had more effect on picture understanding than did art style. But it makes sense that those

9. A study of how the ten key measures correlated with each other suggested that understanding skills fall into a hierarchy of interdependence. For instance, whatever affects the scores for skills at the top (global understanding and temporal organization) generally affects the scores for the other measures. The measures beneath the top two fall into two subgroups: those that involve recognition (passivity, and closure), and those that involve analogy (chaining, completion, and verb choice). Further study of these correlations is necessary before definitive conclusions can be drawn.

who worked at traditional occupations in more isolated areas and who had less formal education, less contact with Western culture, and less experience with pictures would score lower.

The most important conclusion from these findings was that art style and content do make a difference in picture understanding, but only after one considers the subjects' environment, sociological background, personal interests, and needs.

And yet, despite the fact that our measures performed well on tests for validity and reliability, we were still criticized for violating key rules of Western research. Some insisted that whatever the local conditions, the sample could have been random. Others argued that the measures could have been harder even though this would have made the subjects seem less skilled in picture communication.

In such cross-cultural studies as ours, there seems to be no open-and-shut case about methodology. Any review of literature reveals tension between the classical paradigm of academic research and an approach that is more in tune with cross-cultural realities. The only question I would pose is this: Is it more important to create an island of tightly controlled research conditions using questions difficult enough to put scores into what researchers would call a "parametric bell-shaped distribution"? Or is it more important to simply measure skill in the context that you find it? Having attempted to square the classical paradigm against cross-cultural realities, I would contend there surely must be a way to strike a compromise between these extremes.

6   Rules of Thumb

Findings from the 423 interviews are rich in what they imply for development communicators about how to improve pictures for traditional areas like Papua New Guinea. Included below are nine rules of thumb that the findings suggest.[1] Also listed are rules of thumb derived from additional research studies on picture communication.

The first three rules of thumb focus on content.

1. Sociological and educational differences have the most effect on picture understanding.

Our Papua New Guinea study showed that while content and style certainly influence picture communication success, it is even more important to consider the viewers' sociological and educational background. For example, it may be feasible to produce a successful picture series on fishing or making canoes, but such pictures might fail to communicate with Bedouin people in North Africa simply because these people live in a desert where fishing and boats are uncommon.

---

1. For another summary of rules of thumb derived from the Papua New Guinea project, see Bruce L. Cook, "Picture Communication in Papua New Guinea," *Educational Broadcasting International* 13, no. 2 (1980), pp. 78-83.

Similarly, a picture series showing how to write and post letters might succeed visually, but mean little to nonliterate people in isolated areas of Papua New Guinea. The need to consider viewer experience might seem obvious, and yet it is common in the West to ignore cultural differences in the hope of reaching the mass audience.

In traditional areas of the world, this practice results in communications that work best with people in the cities. If media workers hope to go beyond the city environment and communicate with rural people, it is usually necessary for them to make the extra effort of becoming familiar with those people before trying to create development messages for them.

2. Pictures of people should be used because they are easily understood.

One unexpected finding was that picture understanding is egocentric. That is, people understand pictures better when the pictures are about people. When we were in Papua New Guinea, we discovered that many literacy primers and other texts for new readers used illustrations of local plant and animal life as a way to adapt content to the local setting. Our research suggests that pictures of people should be used instead. Slightly more difficult to recognize are "extensions of man" (hands, arms, legs, tools, or weapons). Still more difficult to recognize are objects in the surrounding environment, especially those that have inherent movement such as a fire or a waterfall.

3. Picture content affects understanding more than art style.

It was clear from our research that content (what the picture is about) has more influence on understanding than how the picture is made (art style). Though detailed black-and-white drawings did produce higher scores for recognition, verb choice, and global understanding, and though photographs produced higher scores for completion, the content variable had still more effect on picture understanding.

This finding has been confirmed by the recent trend in

thematic investigation (see chapter 7), which suggests that socially relevant themes increase understanding in pictures. The implication is that publishers must be sensitive to the needs of the local people when selecting content to be used.

For example, rather than picture a fat cat on a mat like a British literacy primer once did in Liberia, a publisher should zero in on a more socially relevant theme, such as contrasting conditions between a family that is sensitive to good hygiene and one that is not. Other locally controversial topics can be discussed with sensitivity in pictures.

The next three rules of thumb focus on art style.

4. Art style does affect preference.

Though art style does not affect understanding as much as content or other factors, it still affects what people like. For this reason, an art style that is popular in a local area should be used to stimulate sales and motivate interest in published materials.

In our study, subjects preferred color over every other art style. The practical implication is that if publishers in Papua New Guinea have a choice, they should use color in their publications. It should be made clear, however, that the extra expense of color can be justified on the basis of preference, not understanding.

One way to cut color costs would be to print a four-color cover with the rest of the publication in black and white. This solution has been used successfully in various locations. It is important to note, though, that if publishers do opt for color, they must keep in mind that colors are usually loaded with cultural meanings. For instance, in some areas of the world, you would not put a yellow cover on a Bible because in that culture yellow connotes sickness and famine.

If color cannot be used for whatever reason, then, according to our research, detailed black-and-white drawings would be the next choice, followed by black-and-white photographs, faceless outline drawings, and, in last place, stick figures. Naturally, as said earlier, preferences in our test could have been influenced by the quality of the art itself.

5. No single art style is best for nonliterate people.

Nowhere in our study did the findings unanimously point to a "best" art style for nonliterate people. However, one minor difference can be detected between findings for the nonliterate subjects and the literate subjects. For the nonliterate subjects, an additional measure—passivity—was affected. The presence of the watercolor wash over the drawings actually distracted nonliterate subjects, increasing their tendency to use passive verbs such as "holding," "standing," and "sitting." This suggests that extraneous details, such as color, do distract nonliterate people from recognizing actions in a picture.[2]

6. If an artist had to choose art style on the basis of this study, realistic art (detailed black-and-white line drawings) would seem best.

Three of ten measures—global understanding, recognition, and verb choice—pointed to detailed black-and-white line drawings as most effective in communicating with nonliterate people.

The last three rules of thumb derived from our research consider comic book usage, pictures that depict lapse of time, and pictures in a series.

7. Publication and distribution of comic book pictures can help develop understanding.

Comic books and picture materials should be marketed early in the development of local literature.[3] Experience with pictures, especially comic books, helps people to develop picture communication skills. This early literature should be viewed as pre-

2. For further information on color as a help or hindrance in picture communication, see David Giltrow, "When Is a Picture Not Worth a Thousand Words?" *Read* 12, no. 1 (January 1977), pp. 28-29.

3. For further information on the use of comic books in teaching, see Emma Halstead Swain, "Using Comic Books to Teach Reading and Language Arts," *Journal of Reading* 22, no. 3 (1978), pp. 253-258. For information on religious applications, see André Knockaert and Chantal van der Plancke, "Bible Comics and Catechesis," *Lumen Vitae: International Review of Religious Education* 34, nos. 2-3 (1979).

reading instruction, rather than a way to turn profits, and so it should be provided at little or no cost to the reader. The content should be locally relevant, not unethical or violent.

8. Avoid using a single picture to depict a lapse of time.

Comics and other pictures in series can communicate a progression of time in a story sequence (at least after someone instructs the people on the correct order for reading the pictures). However, using a single picture to convey a lapse of time should be avoided. In this study, many subjects could not think of a verb in response to a single frame intended to depict cornstalks in the process of growing.

9. Do not assume that viewers automatically recognize a cause and effect relationship between two pictures.

Subjects in our study tended to view each picture in a story as a specific "now" moment in time, unrelated to pictures that preceded or followed it. For example, some subjects found it hard to discern that the man carrying materials in one frame of a picture series was the one who had built the house depicted in a subsequent frame. In another context, two pictures—the first showing a mother nursing a baby and the second showing the baby in good health—might not be enough information to communicate the intended causal relationship between breast feeding and health.

In both cases, related past or future actions will be recognized more easily with supplementary instructions or with an increased number of pictures in the series.

Rules of thumb derived from other research studies

A study of research literature in general reveals other rules of thumb, which, according to the various researchers and writers, help to make pictures more easily understood by traditional people.[4] These additional rules of thumb are listed below ac-

4. This listing was derived from a review of 91 field research studies. See Bruce L. Cook, "Effective Use of Pictures in Literacy Education," pp. 1-55.

cording to their frequency of occurrence in research publications, beginning with those most frequently cited.[5]

1. Realism. Use realistic pictures. This usually means culturally accurate detailed line drawings with natural proportions and, if applicable, natural color. Some examples of unrealistic pictures are a blue tree with orange bananas, or enlargements of insects and rodents that make traditional people say, "We don't have big bugs or rats like that here."

2. Detail. Include only features that are essential in communicating the intended message. (This set of choices will govern the choice between simple, detailed, and complex art styles.)

3. Relevance. Use familiar pictures that have some relevance to the viewer's daily life and interests. If viewing the picture will somehow help viewers escape from oppressive forces, they'll more likely understand the picture. (This is perhaps the reason that picture communication studies are of such interest to religious and political groups.)

4. Color. Consider whether the increased cost of color is justified by viewer reaction (preference, understanding, or sales).

5. Pictures in a series. If a series of pictures is called for, find some way to communicate the order in which the pictures should be viewed. Sometimes a verbal explanation is possible.

6. Background. Enhance the separation between figure and background, provided this will not detract from communication success.

7. Position on page. If possible, ascertain the most popular position on the page and put the picture in that position.

8. Abstractions. Avoid using abstract symbols and maps.

9. Status. Try to discern whether photographs or drawings might have higher status among the intended viewers.

10. Action. Avoid using pictures that require subjects to understand the movement being depicted such as a crackling fire or a speeding bicycle.

11. Art and copy. Be careful of the balance between art,

---

5. As mentioned earlier, we tried to incorporate these principles into our set of stimulus pictures.

text, and captions, as needed. All three should enhance each other.

12. Information limit. Limit the number of objects and actions in each picture.[6]

Putting the rules of thumb to work

Media coordinators can train local message designers to apply the rules of thumb to their own products. This encourages artists, publishers, and others to improve pictures by implementing sound research findings.

A valuable resource to use in this context would be *Illustrations for Development,* a training manual for artists launched by UNICEF, the Centre for Continuing Education at the University of Zambia, and Afrolit Society.[7] The manual and accompanying syllabus emphasize practical guidance for artists as they develop pictures for rural readers.

The plan calls for the manual to be pretested in Zambia in southern Africa, Uganda in East Africa, and one other country in west Africa.

After pretesting, it will be made available to literacy education projects in the three designated countries. If the evaluation is generally positive, the manual will be revised and then made available for use with artists in other areas of Africa. If successful, the manual could be used as a model for developing similar programs in other areas of the world. For further information, write to William Nkunika, P.O. Box RW516, Ridgeway, Lusaka, Zambia or Charles T. Hein, General Secretary, Afrolit Society, P.O. Box 72511, Nairobi, Kenya.

6. This list omits another 21 factors that affect picture communication but do not appear as frequently in the literature. Several examples are viewing time, positiveness of content, human figure representation, "split-representation" (where both sides of an object are shown at once as in early cave drawings), polyphasic pictorial perception (seeing a progression of events in a single picture), local vs. commercial art source, humor, use of shading, figural cutoffs (where another figure or the edge of the picture cuts off a part of a figure), similarity to traditional art, and use of wide shot vs. close-up in pictures.

7. George McBean, Norbert Kaggwa, John Bugembe, eds., *Illustrations for Development: A Manual for Cross-Cultural Communication through Illustration and Workshops for Artists in Africa* (Nairobi, Kenya: Afrolit Society, 1980).

For further reference

Information on picture communication studies in other traditional areas of the world can be obtained at the following addresses.

1. Afrolit Society
P.O. Box 72511
Nairobi, Kenya

2. Association for Educational
Communications and Technology
1126 16th St., N.W.
Washington, DC 20036, USA

3. Center for International
Education
School of Education
Hills House South
University of Massachusetts
Amherst, MA 01003, USA

4. Centre for the Study of
Education in Changing Societies
Badhuisweg 251, P.O. Box 90734
2509 LS The Hague
The Netherlands

5. *Educational Broadcasting
International (EBI Journal)*
British Council
Tavistock House South
Tavistock Square
London WC1H 9LL, England

6. The Ford Foundation,
International Division
320 East 43rd Street
New York, NY 10017, USA

7. Lesotho Distance
Teaching Centre
P.O. Box MS 781
Maseru, Lesotho

8. *Read Magazine*
Summer Institute of Linguistics
Ukarumpa, Via Lae
Papua New Guinea

9. UNESCO
7 Place de Fontenoy
75700 Paris, France

10. UNICEF
P.O. Box 44145
Nairobi, Kenya or
P.O. Box 1187
Katmandu, Nepal

7 Suggestions for Future Research Projects

Those involved in picture communication are the first to point out that rules of thumb can be helpful but may not apply in every setting. For this reason the following simple methods are presented to help development communicators conduct their own research. In this way, they will be able to uncover information about local picture communication problems that may not have been covered either in our 1975 Papua New Guinea study or in other studies around the world.

The methods that follow can be implemented on the job, with fieldwork that should require a time frame of only one or two days.

Things to do before the research

Before launching a project, development communicators should take four steps:

1. Find out if there is a problem.

To ascertain research needs for any geographic area, ask whether there is a problem of picture communication in the first place. In my experience, local artists simply do not know. If, during the pressing demands of the day, they question whether a picture of a brown hand pressing down piano keys doesn't look more like a taro root on black and white slats, where can they get an outside opinion? Usually, their only recourse is to ask their friends in the pressroom or other contacts in the city. Because they have not visited the local area for some time, they have no way of knowing how villagers will interpret their picture of a hand playing the piano.

Ideally, development communicators should take the time to go out to the villagers and discover on a firsthand basis what the villagers do or do not understand. If a problem is discovered then perhaps a simple research project is necessary. However, step 2 below should be considered first.

2. Determine how much has already been done.

Further research can usually be justified for almost any area, and yet it is still important to begin by asking how much has already been done. (For example, see Appendix 2 for summary of picture communication research in Papua, New Guinea, 1898-1975.) Development communicators dealing with isolated areas in India or Latin America might make a case for further research. On the other hand, media coordinators working with projects in Kenya might despair at the very thought of further picture communication research.[1]

3. Develop a workable interview.

If a problem in picture understanding is discovered, and if current research has not touched on the particular problem, the next step is to develop a workable interview.

First of all, study chapters 1—5 of this monograph in order to become familiar with what is involved in the interview process. This practical summary of live field experience should begin to answer such questions as: what kind of pictures to test,

1. Robert A. LeVine, "An Impossible Dream? The Child Development Research Units of Kenya and Nigeria," *Carnegie Quarterly* 27, no. 4 (1979), pp. 1-7.

what content to include in the pictures, what art styles to test, how long the interview should be, how to conduct the interview, and whom to interview.

Of course, the Papua New Guinea study itself could very well be used as the basis for an interview in a local area. If this is the case, the following should be kept in mind.

First of all, keep the interview simple. It won't be necessary to do such intensive research in most settings. Select just the questions and/or pictures that will help solve your particular problem. In some cases, you may want to replace some of the questions and pictures with ones that more closely fit your situation. For instance, if your artists have had trouble knowing what size to draw small objects, you could prepare pictures of a small creature such as a locust, in at least three sizes: small, medium, and large. You would then present these pictures along with the others and record which size was most easily understood by your viewers.[2]

Second, be sure to update the methods used. Try to implement thematic investigative techniques that have come into vogue since 1975. (These are discussed below.)

Third, adapt the pictures to the culture. For example, in the woodcutter story facial features and clothing were adapted for testing in India:

2. If new photographs need to be tested, it would be worthwhile to consider starting with photographs of homemade dolls or mannequins rather than real actors. The dolls would be staged in the same positions the real actors would take in the final production.

Another simpler interview has been outlined by Jane K. Vella of the Center for International Education at the University of Massachusetts. Her interview incorporates thematic investigation techniques.[3]

Vella suggests showing pictures of local situations that, in her words, are "starkly contrasting" and then asking a standard set of questions:

Socially related questions
a. What do you see happening here?
b. Why does it happen?
c. Does this happen in your situation?
d. If it does, what problems does it cause?
e. What can we together do about it?

These simple questions can be adapted to fit whatever pictures are used.

In one example, Vella contrasts a scene of a robust baby with a picture of an emaciated baby. She then adjusts the questions to read: What do you see here? Why does it happen? Are there poorly nourished babies in your village? What can we together do about this problem?

In another example, she uses a series of three pictures. In the first, a family living in a temporary house is planning to build a permanent house. In the second, the family is building a new house made of sun-dried bricks. In the final picture, the family is eating a meal in the new house.

For these pictures, Vella suggests asking some of these questions: What do you see happening in these pictures? What is responsible for such a change? Is it an expensive business—building a new house? Where did these people get the materials for their new home? How do you think they feel in picture No. 3?

As Vella's examples show, her technique is flexible enough to accommodate local needs. Artists can tailor pictures and questions to deal with fishing methods, building materials, hygiene practices, or other local problems. Such flexibility would be particularly helpful when doing research in politically sensitive areas.

3. Jane Kathryn Vella, *Visual Aids for Nonformal Education*, pp. 24-28.

Vella's insistence on greater social relevance in development pictures is compatible with the current trend in development
communication where materials are developed along themes that
are of immediate concern to intended learners. In some cases, the
learner is invited to participate in creating the material. This
"learner-centered" trend was identified as early as 1956 by W.S.
Gray,[4] but today it is popular to attribute it to the "thematic
investigation" methods of Paulo Freire, a revolutionary Latin
American educator.[5] Thematic investigation, or investigating
socially related themes, represents an update on our 1975
methods and should be implemented in any further research.

Once her five socially related questions are presented, Vella
recommends that the interviewer go on to ask questions that help
measure the viewer's perception of the pictures. Based on some
of her thoughts, here is the sequence of questions I would pro-
pose:

Questions on perception

a. What is happening in this picture?
b. What is this? (repeat question, pointing to different details
   in the picture)
c. Can you find something in this picture that is not clear?
d. Can you tell me how to make it better?
e. Can you think of anything that we forgot to put in the picture?

The first question "What is happening in this picture?" is
the standard opening question to use in picture communication
research.[6] There is general agreement on its usefulness and on its
neutrality in introducing the analysis.

The second question "What is this?" is a backup to test the

4. William S. Gray, *The Teaching of Reading and Writing: An International Survey*
(Chicago: Scott, Foresman and Co., 1956), pp. 87-93.

5. Paulo Freire, "Education as the Practice of Freedom," *Education for Critical Con-
sciousness,* ed. and trans. Myra Bergman Romas (New York: Seabury Press, 1973), pp.
3-84. See also Gerald H. Maring, "Freire, Gray, and Robinson on Reading," *Journal of
Reading* 21, no. 5 (February 1978), pp. 421-425.

6. For example, see Philip L. Kilbride and Michael C. Robbins, "Linear Perspective,
Pictorial Depth Perception and Education among the Baganda," *Perceptual and Motor
Skills* 27 (October 1968), p. 601.

validity of the answers to the first question. It is repeated for various details in the picture.

Another way to check validity would be to apply the same two questions to a collection of pictures, half of which had a perceptual ambiguity say, border cutoffs, and half of which did not. A border cutoff occurs where a figure is cut off by the frame line, something that might be seen as an amputation, such as the hunter's legs in this frame from our killing-the-pig sequence.

If, during the interview, perceptual problems arose for the border cutoff pictures but not for the others, then the investigator would know with some validity that border cutoffs did confuse the villagers interviewed.

A third way to test validity was suggested by John Sievert of the Lutheran Mission in New Guinea. Sievert began with the question "What do you see?" for each picture, but then backed it up by asking subjects to rank the pictures according to "how effectively the subject thought they portrayed the basic contents of the picture."

As these examples indicate, validity checks do not have to resort to complicated statistical tests. More likely, they will be

logical, commonsense tests in which development communicators check to be sure there is a consistency between
questions or between similar pictures.[7]

The remaining three questions on Vella's list are usually
difficult for subjects to answer. But it is worthwhile giving them a
try, partly because some will give useful answers and also partly
because by asking such questions, the interviewer shows respect
for the subjects' opinions.

4. Discuss completed interview format with associates.

This is the final step before the research project is launched.
Be aware that unless all proposed users of the research findings
are fully consulted during development of the project, they may
oppose it during fieldwork and effectively prevent its application.
Obviously, if it is found that no action will be taken after research
findings are in, then the research plans should either be scrapped
or applied to the development of a more effective strategy for the
future. Among the things to discuss with users are basic pur-
poses, costs of sampling, money already spent, the need for the
research, and specific ways findings might be implemented in
actual publications.

Putting the research interview to work

Following are suggestions that apply to the actual interview
situation.

1. Choose the appropriate interviewer.

Anyone on the publisher's staff can conduct the interviews,
including the publisher. More than likely, the interviewer will be
the artist. We found that using an indigenous worker to conduct
the research—as opposed to an outsider—creates far less tension
in the interview setting.

7. For a listing of validity problems that go beyond this analysis, see Gordon C. Whiting
and Gerald Hursh-Cesar, "Types of Field Experiments," *Third World Surveys: Survey
Research in Developing Nations,* ed. Gerald Hursh-Cesar and Prodipto Roy (Delhi, India:
Council for Social Development, 1976), pp. 141-187.

2. *Select representative subjects and respect the local culture.*

It is never enough to interview one typical villager. After all, who is typical? Our experience confirmed that when you ask for a typical villager, the people usually lead you to the best educated person in the area. At other times, typical villagers will volunteer themselves, but they may turn out to be gamblers who have just quit the day's gaming in front of the local trade store. (This actually happened to us once.)

There should be at least enough interviews so that the investigator can begin to see some repetition in the villagers' reactions. A safe number might lie anywhere between 10 and 30.

If random subject selection for the interviews is possible without violating cultural norms, fine. Otherwise, don't worry about random sampling. In the same way, evaluate whether it is culturally acceptable to interview in private. In making these decisions, it is of utmost importance to respect local norms and leadership patterns.

3. *Take notes.*

During the interview, some kind of response record must be kept. This is important because even the most accomplished researchers forget what they've heard after doing ten interviews. Notes can be taped on a cassette recorder or scrawled on loose sheets of paper. Suggestions for tabulating and scoring responses from research interviews are given in Appendix 1 on page 99. These suggestions will be especially helpful for those who need to conduct a large number of interviews.

4. *Classify the subjects.*

Demographic details should be recorded: age, sex, education, occupation, geographic area, and formal education or literacy. As names are added to the interview list, such questions as, "Do older people understand better than younger people?" and "Does formal education make a difference in how well villagers understand pictures?" become crucial in the final analysis.

Without such measures, investigators have no way of

knowing whether the score was high because they interviewed too many young, educated men in the city, or whether the details in the pictures were only difficult for a certain subgroup of people, say, older uneducated women who worked at traditional occupations.

Generally, it is better to measure extra data at first and then drop it from analysis later. That way, if one of the measures fails, then another can take up the slack. As seen earlier, what is working here is a system of backup validity checks.

5. Repeat the interview cycle as often as needed.

In the case of Vella's interview, the first cycle opens with her five socially related questions, continues with the questions about perception, and concludes with questions on background details. Responses should then be tabulated. After that, create the pictures and revise them if necessary according to the answers and observations received. Return to the same subjects, but ask just the perceptual questions over again. Revise pictures if needed. This cycle is repeated over and over for whatever interview is used until the pictures are satisfactory to the interviewer and the subjects.

How the methods apply in an actual situation

To visualize how a research interview might work in an actual situation, one can imagine that one is an artist who is visiting the village of Barili in the Philippines. This was where I first did picture interviews in 1974. We'll assume for the sake of illustration, that the villagers have had trouble understanding pictures in how-to-do-it pamphlets on new fishing methods. A study of research has turned up very little information on this problem for this area.

As we launch the project, we plan to stay in the village at least two days. Upon arrival, we establish a point of contact: a government person, an educator, a trade store clerk or owner, a family, or a village elder. At this time, we arrange for a translator and a place to talk with the villagers.

On the morning of the first day, we begin the task of

thematic investigation. That is, we simply try to get a feeling for what the villagers think of the modern fishing methods being imposed by the government. This was the concern of the villagers when I visited Barili in 1974.[8]

We greet a group of workers constructing blue outriggers for ocean fishing, and, with the help of a translator, strike up a conversation with the foreman of the crew. During the course of the first hour, they admit that they are upset about the new fishing methods the government wants them to use. We find out as much as we can about how the new methods compare with the old.

At some point in the morning, we draw pictures of what we've heard about the fishing methods—perhaps illustrating old methods alongside new. We then show them to the foreman and his workers.

During the discussion, without using a clipboard or questionnaire, we subtly apply our adaptation of Vella's list of five socially related questions. (We'll use her interview here for the sake of illustration.) The questions might run like this: What do you see happening in these pictures? What is responsible for such a change? What would it cost to go from the old fishing methods to the new? What are the advantages of the old way? What are the advantages of the new way? How do you think the people feel in the last picture?

As soon as the socially related questions have been asked, we proceed to the questions on perception. These can be asked in the group context or in visiting individuals at work.

That night we apply what we've heard during the day to a new set of sketches. We might prepare three picture pairs depicting old fishing versus new fishing. Or we might sketch pairs of pictures depicting how the village and its people look now versus a more positive scene of how they would look if they adopted the new procedures.

The next day, we show the pictures to each of ten workers

---

8. Since I was not using Vella's thematic investigation approach in those days, I did not adapt my pictures to this concern. Instead, I displayed some pictures the United Bible Society had asked me to test along with some Bible story pictures I'd brought with me from the U.S. Perhaps I would have gotten more response if I had touched on this more relevant issue.

and go through only the list of perceptual questions. (What is happening in this picture? What is this? Can you find something in this picture that isn't clear? Can you tell me how to make it better? Can you think of anything that we forgot to put in the picture?)

If all ten workers say the pictures are fine, we can then revert to the backup question: "What is this?" and point to different details in the picture. This is our validity check.

We might find that for at least a third of the pictures, six of the ten workers said extraneous things when we pressed them to identify specific details. If they missed at least one-third of these recognitions, we can go to them to find out what was wrong. If we find that the subjects are too old to fish, so opposed to the new methods that they are angry, or saturated with betel nuts and beer, we might leave our pictures as they are.

But if further questions reveal that the pictures are confusing, we attempt to discover which perceptual ambiguities the pictures have in common. For example, we might find that pictures of fish aren't recognized when the outline of the fish is cut off by the surrounding visual context, such as the spray from the boat's wake, a fishing net, or the boat's gunwale. Perhaps exploded diagrams of the new fishing rod simply didn't communicate the idea of separate parts, or maybe an enlarged picture of a fishhook looked too much like an anchor or pickax.

Such findings would help us pinpoint the problem. However, solutions to the problem will not be inherent in the research unless a more effective picture can be included in the stimulus set.

For example, if the fish isn't recognized when it is cut off by its visual context (boat, water, net), should we draw it in full, in midair, out of water? How will the fishermen react? Or, once we solve that problem, how can we better identify the parts of the rod? Finally, is there a ratio that will prevent enlarging figures such as a fishhook beyond appropriate size? (See rules of thumb, page 84.) In order to find solutions to these questions, we have to incorporate into the pictures a test of how subjects respond to the different ways a fish, a rod, and a hook are portrayed.

Of course, there's always the slim chance that all scores will be perfect and all validity checks will be successful. If this occurs, we will know that our pictures are communicating effectively.

Regardless of the outcome, the results of two days' research in the village will certainly prove worthwhile. If nothing else, we will return to the office with a clearer idea of how to prepare more socially relevant pictures, and how to adjust our art techniques to communicate more effectively in a rural setting.

Certainly we could use the findings in preparing future how-to-do-it pamphlets. Perhaps we can even share the findings with other artists through correspondence and newsletter articles circulated by the local project facilitator or media coordinators at more regional levels.

A well-balanced design

Hopefully, research projects in the future can take advantage of the methods outlined here. The attempt has been to steer a course between academic research that has been too concerned with methodology for its own sake, and hands-on field studies that have sometimes cut too many corners.

In planning research, development communicators need to find for themselves a way to avoid an academic approach that is rigid and inconsiderate of local realities and an impromptu approach, which, though it has common sense, is patently invalid. What is really needed today and in the future is a meeting of these two approaches, an attempt to make the academic approach practical and relevant, and the quick, commonsense approach more valid and reliable.

Appendix 1

Scoring Responses from a Research Interview

The following illustration will demonstrate one way of computing percentage scores from interview responses.

In a hypothetical research interview, subjects were asked to recognize household items in pictures. A tally of their scores is included below. Note that subjects were classified by area (A, B, C, or D), by literacy, and by age. Note also that in each of these subsets, seven interviews were conducted. Perfect score for each interview was 4 points. Points were lost as subjects failed to recognize items in the pictures.

Tally of scores for recognition of household items

	Area A	Area B	Area C	Area D
Literate				
Age 15-50	4,4,4,4	4,4,3,3	4,4,3,2	3,2,4,4
	3,4,3	4,3,4	3,4,3	3,4,3
Age 51 plus	3,3,3,4	4,3,2,4	4,4,3,4	3,3,2,3
	4,3,3	3,2,4	2,4,2	2,3,2
Nonliterate				
Age 15-50	3,2,3,2	3,2,3,4	3,4,2,3	3,2,2,2
	4,2,3	2,3,2	2,2,2	3,2,2
Age 51 plus	3,2,3,2	3,2,3,4	3,4,2,3	2,1,1,1
	3,2,3	3,2,2	3,2,2	3,2,2

After scores from the interviews have been tallied as in the above example, it is possible to add up scores in each subset. *Example:* In the top left subset, the scores (4,4,4,4,3,4,3) are added to total 26. After this has been done for each subset, add the totals across and down for each variable. Answers can be verified with the results below:

**Subset totals
for area, literacy, and age
in recognition of household items**

	Area A	Area B	Area C	Area D	Total Score
Literate					
Age 15-50	26	25	23	23	97
Age 51 plus	23	22	23	18	86
Overall literate	49	47	46	41	183
Nonliterate					
Age 15-50	19	19	18	16	72
Age 51 plus	18	19	19	11	67
Overall nonliterate	37	38	37	27	139
Total score	86	85	83	68	322

Next note the maximum possible number of points that could have been achieved in each subset and compute the percentage score for each one. *Example:* The percentage score for the top left subset is 93% because 26, the number scored, is 93% of the maximum score of 28. (There were 7 interviews with a possible 4 points perfect score for each interview.) For the above tally, the results are as follows:

**Percentage computations for recognition
tally by area, literacy, and age**

	Area A	Area B	Area C	Area D	Overall
Literate					
Age 15-50	93%	89%	82%	82%	87%
Age 51 plus	82%	79%	82%	64%	77%
Overall literate	87%	84%	82%	73%	82%
Nonliterate					
Age 15-50	68%	68%	64%	57%	64%
Age 51 plus	64%	68%	68%	39%	60%
Overall nonliterate	66%	68%	66%	48%	62%
Overall (literacy, age)	77%	76%	74%	61%	72%

This hypothetical tally shows that literates outperformed nonliterates 82% to 62%, that older people had slightly lower scores whether they were literate or not, and that Area D had lower scores. Note that other percentages could be computed from the numbers in this table, and other variables (such as content and art style) could be broken down similarly.

Appendix 2

Picture Communication Studies in Papua New Guinea: 1898—1975

W. H. R. Rivers and the Cambridge Anthropological Expedition

Papua New Guinea was the site of the very first recorded picture communication research, the Cambridge Anthropological Expedition to the Torres Straits in 1898.[1] On that trip, Rivers, a British psychologist, found that the people in the Fly River area understood pictures well.[2] He also noted that the people might have been more interested in pictures of local people. (Rivers' realistic pictures depicted two Western people—a man and a boy).[3] Unfortunately, too many later studies in New Guinea and Africa failed to heed this finding and truly adapt pictures to the local culture in the test areas.

Finally, Rivers cited language difficulty in his interviews with the English expressions "close up" and "far away."[4]

Rivers is significant because he was the very first in the field of picture communication research.[5] Not only did he wrestle with the problems of language, but he considered optical illusions, understanding, preferences, and even research methods. His is the first formulation of what later came to be

1. A. C. Haddon, ed., *Reports of the Cambridge Anthropological Expedition to Torres Straights*, 6 vols. (London: Cambridge University Press, 1901).

2. W. H. R. Rivers, "Vision," *Physiology and Psychology*, vol. 2, *Reports of the Cambridge Expedition*, p. 130.

3. Ibid.

4. Rivers, pp. 97-98. See also page 63 in this monograph and Cook, *Understanding Pictures in Papua New Guinea*, 1978, pp. 198-200, 300-310.

5. L. L. Langness and Thomas Gladwin, "Oceania," *Psychological Anthropology*, 2d ed., ed. Francis L. L. Hsu (Cambridge, Mass.: Shenkman Publishing Co., 1972), p. 170.

called studies of pictorial perception, or picture communication.[6]

Ellis Silas and *The Primitive Arcadia*

After Rivers, the next researcher to arrive in Papua New Guinea was Ellis Silas, a Western artist, who wrote a study in 1926 with the title: *A Primitive Arcadia: Being the Impressions of an Artist in Papua*. Silas simply walked around Papua drawing pictures, showing them to the local people, and then recording his amazement at how well the people could understand them.[7] Silas' story is refreshing, as very few studies take this positive approach. Too often the researcher focuses on perceptual failures, not success.

Margaret Mead in Papua New Guinea

By 1930 anthropologist Margaret Mead had begun using pictures to study culture in Papua New Guinea.[8] She listened as local youth told stories to go along with some pictures she showed them. However, she only listened for cultural details in their responses. We had to set aside her excellent work and a few others for our own study because they focused on culture, not communication success.

Reports of Berndt and Forge

In more recent studies not everyone agreed that villagers in Papua New Guinea understood pictures well. A contrary impression originated in 1959 when anthropologist Catherine H. Berndt published an article on pictures used in certain cultural ceremonies in Papua New Guinea and made a point of mentioning that the people couldn't interpret them.[9] This anecdotal finding would have passed without notice, except that Anthony Forge repeated her point of view in a 1970 publication, commenting that local people had trouble understanding photographs.[10]

As a result of Berndt's and Forge's reports, Western researchers developed the tendency to look down their noses at Papua New Guineans, who supposedly could not understand pictures. A similar situation had already developed in

---

6. *Picture communication* is the process of sharing or exchanging something (information, emotion, humor) through pictures.

7. Ellis Silas, *A Primitive Arcadia: Being the Impressions of an Artist in Papua* (London: T. Fisher Unwin, 1926), p. 207.

8. Margaret Mead, *Growing Up in New Guinea* (1930; reprint ed., New York: Mentor Books, 1961), pp. 159-161; idem, *New Lives for Old: Cultural Transformation–Manus, 1928-1953* (New York: William Morrow and Co., 1956), pp. 353-354, 367, 490.

9. Catherine H. Berndt, "Ascription of Meaning in a Ceremonial Context, in the Eastern Highlands of New Guinea," *Anthropology in the South Seas,* ed. John Derek Freedman and William Robert Geddes (New Plymouth, New Zealand: Thomas Avery, 1959), pp. 161-183.

10. Anthony Forge, "Learning to See in New Guinea," *Socialization: The Approach from Social Anthropology* (London: Tavistock Publications, 1970), pp. 269-291.

Africa where early psychologists first used pictures in the study of racial differences.[11]

Studies from *Read* magazine

Read magazine published by Summer Institute of Linguistics (Ukarumpa, Papua New Guinea) has offered several useful articles on picture communication research in Papua New Guinea.

The very first issue of *Read* in September, 1966, reported on illustration research by John Sievert of the Lutheran Mission.[12] Sievert mailed a wide variety of pictures to missionaries, who then tested them with local people of differing educational background.

Although the data analysis was never completely reported, several observations did emerge, including the following (condensed): (a) photographs have higher "prestige value"; (b) people with more formal education see more details; (c) literate people state preferences more confidently and have a broader range of expectations about the kind of subjects pictures can depict; (d) "simple and realistic" illustrations communicate best; (e) a careful balance between illustration, caption, and text is important; (f) clear and uncluttered photographs are understood, as are realistic and color outline drawings; (g) stick figures and "two-dimensional outline drawings" are not understood well; (h) the same types of pictures work equally well in different geographical settings; (i) the addition of a second color in printing isn't worth the cost in terms of increased understanding.

The specificity of this listing sets it apart from Forge's 1970 report that local people couldn't understand photographs. Here was something that local publishers could actually use in their work, and it didn't demean the people, either.

Two other *Read* studies were by Roy Gwyther-Jones, current director of media for Wycliffe Bible Translators, Australia. From 1967 field tests of various tints, Gwyther-Jones advised generally that detailed drawings could be recognized as pictures of white people, while silhouettes could be seen as "spirits of (the) dead."[13] In 1968 he published a listing of rules of thumb for using photographs in publications.[14] The same issue included eight rules for artists, reprinted from another publication.[15]

---

11. See, for example, H. W. Nissen, S. Machover, and Elaine F. Kinder, "A Study of Performance Tests Given to a Group of Native African Negro Children," *The British Journal of Psychology* 35, no. 3 (January 1935), pp. 308-355; W. M. Beveridge, "Racial Differences in Phenomenal Regression," *The British Journal of Psychology* 26, no. 1 (July 1935), pp. 51-64.

12. John Sievert, "Illustration Research," *Read* 1, nos. 1-3 (1966), p. 8. This was reprinted as "Illustration Research '66," *Read* 5, no. 1 (1970), pp. 22-23.

13. Roy Gwyther-Jones, "Tints," *Read* 2, no. 2 (1967), p. 13. Never in 423 interviews, where I used faceless outline figures in a wide variety of geographical areas, did I hear one mention of spirits.

14. Roy Gwyther-Jones, "Photographs for Reproduction," *Read* 3, no. 2 (1968), pp. 12-13.

15. "Artists Advise Editors," *Read* 3, no. 2 (1968), p. 13. This was a reprint of "Artists Advise Editors," *The Word at Work*, 1962.

In 1972 a Nipa missionary couple, Ron and Margaret Reeson, published their first article describing how they were able to use stick figures effectively to help the local people remember Bible stories.[16] We visited their mission during our fieldwork to determine whether exposure to stick figures such as theirs would affect reactions to the stick figures we were testing. Though we detected no statistical difference between responses from their area and those obtained elsewhere, it was clear the Reesons had successfully used stick figures as an aid to memory.

In a sequel to her first report published six years later, Margaret Reeson elaborated further that the pictures in her stories required occasional help from a literate person.[17] She also stressed the importance of using an art style that "anybody can draw" so that pastors could draw pictures on the blackboard while teaching.

In 1973 *Read* magazine published a useful article by Ann F. Cates of Summer Institute of Linguistics that described an attempt to determine what kinds of literature local people really wanted.[18] Among other things, Cates reported that Atzera men were more interested than women in pictures of "items outside their immediate environment."

In the January 1977 issue of *Read,* Paul W. Brennan reported on the difficulty he had in choosing well-liked, easily understood Bible illustrations for the Enga people.[19] His first attempt was to print Bible portions alongside Annie Vallotton's faceless line drawings from the Good News Bible. Enga people objected, however, that these pictures were incomprehensible, ambiguous, or culturally irrelevant. When contemporary photographs were used instead, local translation assistants objected to using local people and local scenery to convey a story set in the Holy Land.

Hutton and Ellison: some useful findings

Two Australian psychologists, Malcolm A. Hutton and A. Ellison, completed a helpful survey in which they suggested a middle ground on the amount of detail a picture should include.[20] They contended that a picture could have too much *or* too little detail. (This can be a problem because, as Spaulding observed in 1953, new readers often fixate on one or more details and thus misunderstand the overall picture.) Take, for example, the pictures reproduced here.[21]

16. Margaret Reeson, "Every Picture Tells a Story," *Read* 7, no. 1 (1972), pp. 14-16.

17. Margaret Reeson, "A Sequel to: Every Picture Tells a Story," *Read* 13, no. 1 (1978), pp. 20-21.

18. Ann F. Cates, "What Literature Should I Provide?," *Read* 8, no. 2 (1973), pp. 22-23.

19. Paul W. Brennan, "Incarnational Illustrations: Enga Reactions to Contemporary Photographs," *Read* 12, no. 1 (1977), pp. 34-36.

20. M. A. Hutton and A. Ellison, *Some Aspects of Pictorial Perception amongst Niuginians,* Psychological Services Section, Department of the Public Service Board Research Report no. 1 (Konedobu Territory of Papua and New Guinea, 1970). The authors of this study attributed the idea of having either too much or too little detail to the late Alan C. Holmes, *A Study of Understanding of Visual Symbols in Kenya,* p. 5.

21. This series is excerpted from Bruce L. Cook, "Effective Use of Pictures in Literacy Education: A Literature Review," *Literacy Review,* no. 2 (1980), pp. 14-20, 35-36.

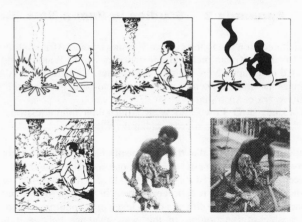

While these pictures range from too little to excess detail, it is clear that the most effective picture is somewhere in between.

Hutton and Ellison's survey included some useful findings. It recommended using familiar objects in pictures for Papuans and New Guineans, and it observed that viewers had no difficulty understanding cues indicating depth in pictures. In addition, the study asserted that viewers saw pictures concretely and literally, without appreciation for the "metaphoric intent."

"Black versus white" studies

Following Hutton and Ellison's work came a series of controversial "Black versus White" studies. In these studies, various psychologists used high-powered Western techniques to test the skills of local people. Because the tests were not adapted to the local culture, however, they tended to report that Western "white" subjects consistently scored higher than "black" subjects from Papua New Guinea.

For example, a 1970 publication summarized years of work by an Australian psychologist, I. G. Ord, who used pictures and other stimuli to test intelligence in the local schools of Papua New Guinea.[22] Ord worked primarily within the schools, but one day a transportation delay forced him into a rural situation in the highlands.[23]

He decided to test his usual materials with the people there—instructors and recruit trainees at Goroka Police Training Centre as well as a group of students at the Roman Catholic Mission in Minj. Ord reported, however, that his tests "proved virtually impossible to communicate to less sophisticated subjects . . ." It didn't occur to him that his test had failed as utterly as the people. Instead, he assumed that picture communication was impossible, and he made no effort to adapt his pictures and testing methods to the immediate cultural realities. This is a classic example of an expatriate who judges people because of their failure to perform to standards applied from another culture.

Another study, completed by L. A. Waldron and A. J. Gallimore, illustrates what happens when, as in Ord's case, there is no attempt to adapt the

22. I. G. Ord, *Mental Tests for Pre-literates: Resulting Mainly from New Guinea Studies* (London: Ginn and Co., 1970), pp. 38-44, 48-51, 57-66.

23. Ord, pp. 19-20.

picture communication test to the culture.[24] Using a South African stimulus set that had influenced African pictorial perception research, Waldron and Gallimore reported that Papua New Guinea "indigenies," Torres Strait islanders, and aborigines had more difficulty perceiving pictorial depth than did "European" subjects from Australia.

A 1974 study by G. Lewis and W. R. Mulford includes a justification for *not* adapting Western tests to a cross-cultural setting:

> While one must admit that there are justifiable arguments for not transplanting tests of Western origin, if one takes the view that the concepts being measured form part of a set of skills necessary for an individual who is to function effectively in Western society and if one asserts that some citizens of all developing countries need to be capable of functioning in this way, then we believe it is acceptable to measure such concept development with such tests with the aim of assessing performance and using the information to improve that performance in some children at least.[25]

Such an explanation is fine except that, as common sense will indicate, a culturally inaccurate research question is likely to produce a misleading answer.

Lewis and Mulford's study attempted to avoid this dilemma by limiting itself to English-speaking students having at least six years of formal education. However, in their study we still find what D. T. Campbell has called "evidence of the ethnocentric bigotry of a Westerner."[26]

Specifically, Lewis and Mulford were seeking to test the hypothesis that there was a five-year lag between Papua New Guinea and Western children in developing an understanding of time concepts. Originally, their study included a series of pictures depicting two trees growing older. The subjects were asked, "Which tree is older?"[27] In the final version of the study, this task was dropped.

Lewis and Mulford actually admitted that they had dropped the task because it was too "familiar" to the children. As a result, they eliminated the only series of pictures that would have truly tested their hypothesis.

In another misleading study, S. K. Randall in 1974 used three pictures from a Western test of development in religious concepts: a child approaching a

24. L. A. Waldron and A. J. Gallimore, "Pictorial Depth Perception in Papua New Guinea, Torres Strait, and Australia," *Australian Journal of Psychology* 25, no. 1 (1973), pp. 89-92.

25. G. Lewis and W. R. Mulford, "Conservation of Time amongst Papua New Guinean School Children: An Exploratory Study," *Papua New Guinea Journal of Education* 10, no. 2 (1974), p. 20.

26. Donald T. Campbell, "Distinguishing Differences of Perception from Failures of Communication in Cross-cultural Studies," *Cross-cultural Understanding: Epistemology in Anthropology*, ed. F. S. C. Northrop and Helen H. Livingston (New York: Harper & Row, 1964), p. 321.

27. Lewis and Mulford, p. 24.

church door with his or her parents,

a child praying at bedside,

and a child looking at a Bible.[28]

   While the author reported that the pictures were adapted to the local situation, it is clear that the church door, the bed, and at least one hairstyle were Western.

28. S. K. Randall, "A Study of Religious Concepts of Some Papua New Guinean and Expatriate School Children," *Papua New Guinea Journal of Education* 10, no. 1 (1974), pp. 10-20.

For the first picture, subjects were asked, "What do you think the boy (or girl) likes (or does not like) about going to church?" Various questions were asked for the second picture. And, for the third, the question was "What kind of book is the Bible?"

Then the author devised a five-point scale ranging from intuitive to abstract religious thinking, rated the responses, and reported that "at least for the three religious concepts examined, Papua New Guinea children develop at a much slower rate than expatriate children living in Papua New Guinea."

Another "Black versus White" study appeared in 1975, the year Papua New Guinea gained independence from Australia.[29] In this study, M. S. Jackson took an outline picture of a pig, put the letters *PIG* above it (see illustration) and said, "This is the name for pig, this is my own."

The next step was to give subjects another set of the same letters and then have them perform eight tasks related to spelling the word under the drawing. As the experimenter gave subjects three little "letter tablets" (*p, i,* and *g),* he said, "This is your one. You make your one just like my one."

Naturally, the Western children scored higher on all but one of the tests. Once again the local children were the losers, and based on his data, the author recommended that "native" children be taught various concepts: left to right, top vs. bottom, and "internal correctness and sequencing."

The studies just outlined leave the impression that psychologists have little complimentary to say about the picture communication skills of traditional people. In one test after the other, the performance level of one culture predictably lags behind that of the other.

Government's Pilot Study on Pictorial Perception

Other studies have offered direct benefits to people who work with the rural population of Papua New Guinea. In 1971 the government's Department of Information Services and Extension Services did a fairly comprehensive pilot study on pictorial perception among local people in the Central District of what was then called the Territory of Papua New Guinea.[30]

29. M. S. Jackson, "A Comparison of the Behaviour of European and Native Children on Initial Confrontation with Reading Stimuli," *Papua New Guinea Journal of Education* 11, no. 1 (1975), pp. 17-23.

30. [R. Moulik], *A Pilot Study in Perception: Central District. An Extension Project. Pilot Study– Perception of some Aspects of Illustrative Material* (Port Moresby, Papua New Guinea: Department of Information and Extension Services, 1971).

Here is a summary of the published findings, all of which should interest publishers and development communicators.

- Adults and children successfully understood size as a perspective cue.
- Adults and children successfully recognized a partial picture—a man seated behind a desk.
- Neither adults nor children could focus on the major action in a picture having two "centres of attention."
- Both children and adults preferred smaller pictures and pictures whose topic was "positive action" (e.g., pictures of someone helping, rather than hitting, another person).
- Adults preferred line drawings to photographs, and both of these to a "single line drawing"—stick figures with some embellishment.
- Occupation, education, and sometimes age were found to correlate with adult picture-understanding skill.
- Adults in certain occupational, education, or age groups were more likely to interpret pictures accurately.
- Older children were more accurate in understanding pictures, while there was little difference in skill according to whether the child was a boy or a girl.

Kennedy and Ross fieldwork among the Songe

The year Papua New Guinea achieved independence, 1975, also saw the publication of a study by two Canadian professors, John Kennedy, a psychologist, and Abraham Ross, an anthropologist.[31]

This was a radical departure because it minimized the possibility of cultural error through collaboration between a psychologist and an anthropologist in planning the test design and the pictures to use. The actual fieldwork was done during the anthropologist's extended stay among the Songe people.

Because of this, the Kennedy and Ross findings seem unusually trustworthy, despite the small sample size of 38 people. Kennedy and Ross reported that the Songe people were proficient at recognizing outline pictures—both the overall figure and the details within. They did note that some people had difficulty recognizing pictures having inherent movement—pictures of a fire and a river. Only the 14 older subjects seemed to have trouble discerning pictorial depth.

31. John M. Kennedy and Abraham S. Ross, "Outline Picture Perception by the Songe of Papua," *Perception* 4, no. 4 (1975).

Selected Bibliography

Armstrong, B. H. "Illustrations and Book Design." *Publishing for the New Reading Audience: A Report of the Burma Committee of the UNESCO Regional Seminar on the Production of Reading Material for New Literates: Rangoon, Burma, October 28-November 30, 1957,* edited by Seth Spaulding. Rangoon, Burma: The Burma Translation Society, 1958.

Arnheim, Rudolf. *Visual Thinking.* Berkeley: University of California Press, 1969.

Bellahsene, C. *Practical Guide to Functional Literacy: A Method of Training for Development.* Paris: United Nations Educational, Scientific and Cultural Organization, Experimental World Literacy Programme, 1973.

Cook, Bruce L. "Effective Use of Pictures in Literacy Education: A Literature Review." *Literacy Review,* no. 2 (1980), pp. 1-55.

————. "Understanding Pictures in Papua New Guinea, 1975: An Experiment Comparing Style and Content in Sociological, Epistemological, and Cognitive Context." Ph.D. dissertation, Temple University, 1979.

Duncan, Hall F., Gourlay, N., and Hudson, William. *A Study of Pictorial Perception among Bantu and White Primary School Children in South Africa.* Human Sciences Research Council Publication Series, no. 31. Johannesburg: Witwatersrand University Press, 1973.

Endreny, Phyllis. *Pictorial Communication with Illiterates: An Introductory Investigation of the Issues.* New York: Population Resource Center, Ford Foundation, July, 1978.

Fan, Eugene J. *The Healthy Village: An Experiment in Visual Education in West China*. Monographs on Fundamental Education, no. 5. Paris: United Nations Educational, Scientific and Cultural Organization, 1951.

Fuglesang, Andreas. *Applied Communication in Developing Countries: Ideas and Observations*. Uppsala, Sweden: The Dag Hammarskjöld Foundation, 1973.

Hein, Charles T., and Kanyogonya, Keith K., eds. *Rural Press for Village Post-literacy Literature*. Afrolit Paper, no. 5. Nairobi: Afrolit Society, 1979.

Holmes, Alan C. *A Study of Understanding of Visual Symbols in Kenya*. London: Overseas Visual Aids Centre, 1963.

Kennedy, John M. *A Psychology of Picture Perception: Images and Information*. San Francisco: Jossey-Bass Publishers, 1974.

———, and Ross, Abraham S. "Outline Picture Perception by the Songe of Papua." *Perception* 4 (1975), pp. 391-406.

Knockaert, André, and van der Plancke, Chantal. "Bible Comics and Catachesis." *Lumen Vitae: International Review of Religious Education* 34, nos. 2-3 (1979).

Leonard, Ann. *Sin Palabras (Without Words): Printed Materials for People Who Do Not Read*. New York: Cycle Communications, 1979.

Lesotho Distance Teaching Centre. *The Use of Photo strips in Family Planning Education*. Maseru, Lesotho: Lesotho Distance Teaching Centre, 1977.

Mitton, Roger. *Understanding Print: A Survey of People's Ability to Understand Text and Illustrations*. Maseru, Lesotho: Lesotho Distance Teaching Centre, 1976.

O'Bryan, K. G. *Summary of Research Findings for Children's Television Workshop*. New York: Children's Television Workshop, 1975.

Rahman, S. *Response to Visuals in Posters: A Study in Communication*. New Delhi: Indian Institute of Mass Communication, 1971.

Richards, Charles Granston, ed. and comp. *The Provision of Popular Reading Materials*. Monographs on Fundamental Education, no. 12. Paris: United Nations Educational, Scientific and Cultural Organization, 1959.

Rodriguez Bou, Ismael. *Estudio sobre Preferencias y Tipos de Illustraciones* Publicaciones Pedagogicas, series 2, no. 10. Rio Piedras, Puerto Rico: Universidad de Puerto Rico, El Consejo Superior de Ensananza, 1950.

_____ , and Lopez, David Cruz. "An Analysis of Publications for Adults: Puerto Rican Experience." *Fundamental and Adult Education* 6 (January 1954), pp. 19-21.

Roy, T. C. "Posters." *Short Course in Agricultural Information Communication (Production and Utilization of Audiovisual Aids)*. New Delhi: Farm Information Unit, Directorate of Extension, Ministry of Food and Agriculture, Community Development and Cooperation, Government of India, 1969.

Saunders, Denys J. *Visual Communication Handbook: Teaching and Learning Using Simple Visual Materials*. London: Lutterworth Press, 1974.

Shaw, Bernard. *Visual Symbols Survey: Report on the Recognition of Drawings in Kenya*. London: Centre for Educational Development Overseas, African Medical and Research Foundation Incorporating East African Flying Doctor Services, 1969.

Spaulding, Seth. "Research on Pictorial Illustration." *Audiovisual Communication Review 3*, no. 1 (1955), pp. 35-45.

_____ , "Communication Potential of Pictorial Illustrations." *Audiovisual Communication Review* 4, no. 1 (1956), pp. 31-46.

Vella, Jane Kathryn. *Visual Aids for Nonformal Education*. Amherst, Massachusetts: Center for International Education, University of Massachusetts, 1979.

Weber, Hans-Reudi. *The Communication of the Gospel to Illiterates: Based on a Missionary Experience in Indonesia*. International Missionary Council Research Pamphlet, no. 4. London: SCM Press, 1957.

Zimmer, Anne, and Zimmer, Fred. *Visual Literacy in Communication: Designing for Development*. Literacy in Development: A Series of Training Monographs, edited by H. S. Bhola. Tehran: International Institute for Adult Literacy Methods, 1978.